D0341185

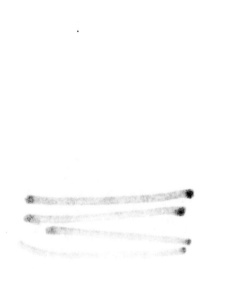

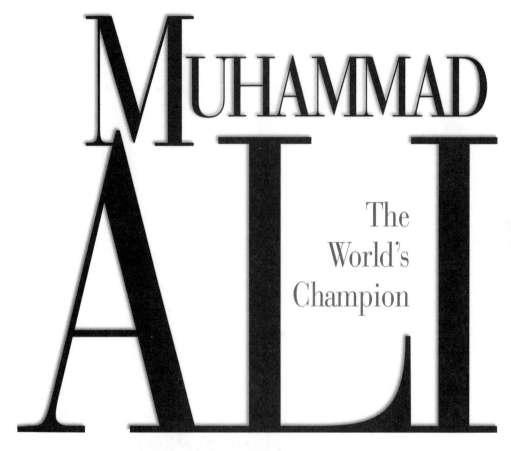

MUHAMMAD ALI

The World's Champion

JOHN TESSITORE

An Impact Biography

FRANKLIN WATTS
A Division of Grolier Publishing
New York London Hong Kong Sydney
Danbury, Connecticut

For my grandfather Frank Tessitore,
a very scientific lover of love
and, incidentally, a boxing fan

And, as always, for my parents, Donna and Joseph;
my sisters, Connie-Lynn and Karyn; and for Kelly

Photographs ©: AllSport USA: 19 (USOC); AllSport USA/Hulton Deutsch: 44, 54, 78; AP/Wide World Photos: 17, 32, 40, 49, 61, 72, 106, 119, 123; Archive Photos/AFP: 87; Archive Photos: 66 (Express Newspapers); Corbis-Bettmann: 6 ,7 (Omar Torres/AFP), cover, 4, 13, 26, 27, 90, 96, 100, 108, 109, 124; SportsChrome East/West: 115 (David Lee Waite).

Visit Franklin Watts on the Internet at:
http://publishing.grolier.com

Library of Congress Cataloging-in-Publication Data
Tessitore, John.
    Muhammad Ali: the world's champion / John Tessitore
        p.   cm. — (An Impact biography)
    Includes bibliographical references and index.
    Summary: A comprehensive biography of the only boxer crowned Heavyweight Champion of the World three times.
    ISBN 0-531-11437-6 (lib. bdg.)   0-531-15927-2 (pbk.)
    1. Ali, Muhammad, 1942–   —Juvenile literature. 2. Boxers (Sports)—United States—Biography—Juvenile literature. [1. Ali, Muhammad, 1942– . 2. Afro-Americans—Biography.] I. Title
    GV1132.A44T47   1998
    796.83'092—dc21
    [B]   97–31204
                                               CIP
                                               AC

Contents

Introduction

The Torch

July 1996. Atlanta, Georgia.

The opening ceremonies of the Summer Olympics were drawing to a close. After a seemingly endless march into the brand-new Olympic Stadium, the world's greatest athletes were finally standing together on the infield, each beneath their own flags. And now the world was waiting for the symbolic beginning of the Games: the lighting of the torch that would burn constantly during the tournament.

Upholding tradition, the Olympic governing committee did not announce its selection for torch-lighter. The 85,000 people in the stadium, and the 3.5 billion people around the globe who were watching on television, did not know who would be given the greatest honor in international sports. In the weeks before the Games, the flame used to light the torch was taken on a long journey around the world. It passed across many smaller torches on its way to Atlanta's Olympic Stadium, until it reached the torch of Evander Holyfield—a resident of Atlanta, a bronze medal winner at the 1984 Olympics, and perhaps the best heavyweight boxer of the 1990s. Holyfield carried the flame into the stadium as the crowd erupted with excitement. Holyfield passed the flame to Janet Evans, America's four-time gold medal–winning swimmer who was preparing to compete again in these very Games. Again, the 85,000 spectators cheered wildly. For a moment, it seemed as if the night had reached its climax, as if there could be no more energy in the stadium.

But then he stepped out of the shadows. First there was a gasp, and then a roar.

Muhammad Ali. Some say his face is the most recognized in the world: a gold medalist in the 1960 Olympics, a three-time world heavyweight champion, an international icon. Sportswriter Bert Sugar once said, "Muhammad is one of the few Americans, and certainly the first American athlete ever, to transcend the borders of this country and become an international hero."[1] Few people anywhere can draw a crowd as quickly as Ali, and as Sugar suggests, he is known around the world. Although the crowd at Olympic Stadium had not come to see him specifically this time, the opening ceremony was suddenly *his* show.

Janet Evans passed the flame to the man known as "The Greatest," and everyone watching reacted in some profound, personal way: Most cheered, laughed, or cried, but some were probably outraged. No athlete has ever elicited as many responses as Muhammad Ali. Almost every person, the boxing fan as well as the critic of the sport, has an interpretation of Ali's life, because boxing is only a part of his story.

Ali held the torch in his right hand and lifted it above his head. Decades of competition had taken their toll and

Muhammad Ali lighting the Olympic flame during the opening ceremonies of the 1996 Games in Atlanta

left him physically damaged. Parkinson's syndrome had silenced the arrogant, comic poet once called "The Louisville Lip." His face, the same handsome face that had charmed fans and opponents alike for over thirty years, was frozen in an expressionless stare. His left hand, once the agent of the most feared jab in boxing, trembled incessantly. The fastest feet in sports history now shuffled along at a snail's pace. Yet, with all of his disabilities, Ali stood as a symbol of survival. His presence on the stage in Olympic Stadium was more important than anything he could have done or said.

Of course, even this perfect moment had its complications. Ali always found a way to make his life just a little more interesting. When he leaned over to light the fuse that would carry the flame to the giant torch overhead, nothing happened. In fact, the flame was now rising up toward his hand. "It wouldn't catch," Ali said later. "I looked around. Then I puffed on it. Three billion people, and I look like a fool."[2] He had rehearsed this moment a week earlier, but he had not practiced with real fire. This was new, and Ali knew enough about his own life to expect the unexpected. He kept holding that flame, almost burning himself, until the torch finally ignited. Then the crowd erupted, and Ali stood before them as a champion once again.

In the 1960s, when Ali was the indestructible heavyweight champion of the world, no one could have predicted the excitement he would still generate in his retirement. For many Americans of that decade, Ali was on the wrong side of the truly divisive issues of the age: civil rights and Vietnam. He would not be patient in his struggle for equality in a segregated society, and he would not fight in a war he found immoral. He was loud, boisterous, confrontational, and demanding. Ultimately, he was stripped of his heavyweight title because he would

8

not alter his views. Much of the world respected his stubborn individuality and willingness to stand up for his beliefs. But his own country rejected him. The fact that he was selected to light the torch for the 1996 Olympic Games, in his own country, in a city once paralyzed by racial conflict, was proof that the United States of America had finally made its peace with Muhammad Ali. Perhaps, in a small way, it was also proof that the nation had made its peace with the historical period that Muhammad Ali will forever represent.

President Bill Clinton attended the opening ceremonies in Atlanta. Clinton was a young boy when Muhammad Ali—then known as Cassius Clay—won a gold medal at the 1960 Olympics. He was a teenager in 1964 when Ali, still Clay, defeated Sonny Liston for the heavyweight title. He remembered vividly the years of strife that marked Ali's reign as champion, and he remembered Ali's role in that strife. Ali was the conscience of the nation in those years, and Clinton was now president of the nation that could not afford to forget the 1960s and the lessons learned about civil rights and war. When the opening ceremonies were over, Clinton sought out Ali. As soon as he found "The Champ," Clinton put his hands on Ali's shoulders and said, "They didn't tell me who would light the flame, but when I saw it was you, I cried."[3]

This is Muhammad Ali's story.

1

Cassius

The story begins in 1860, when newly elected President Abraham Lincoln was assembling his administration from the rank and file of the Republican party. High on his list of candidates for office was a Kentucky landholder and politician renowned for his antislavery position: Cassius Marcellus Clay. Clay had inherited a large plantation from his father, staffed with the usual complement of slaves. But as an abolitionist, Clay emancipated his slaves and campaigned against any law that preserved the institution of slavery. For his brave, outspoken defiance of Southern conventions, Clay was threatened with assassination on numerous occasions. He carried a set of pistols and a bowie knife at all times to protect himself against attackers. Lincoln sent Clay to Russia as U.S. ambassador. But among African-Americans, particularly in the state of Kentucky, Clay would always be associated with the hard, perilous fight against slavery. And his name survived among the families of his former slaves. Now, however, Cassius Marcellus Clay's name has a different kind of significance.

On January 17, 1942, in Louisville General Hospital, a baby born was born to an African-American couple, Odessa Grady Clay and her husband Cassius Marcellus Clay. "Cash," as the father was sometimes known, was a billboard and sign painter, the grandson of "free coloreds"—African-Americans who were not slaves. Odessa was a domestic, a maid. On the maternal side of her family, she was the granddaughter of a white man and a slave named Dinah. On the paternal side, her grandfather was an Irish immigrant, and her grandmother a "free colored." Upholding family tradition, the Clays named their firstborn Cassius Marcellus Clay, Jr., and kept the old abolitionist's name alive.

Cash was a good provider. Unlike many other African-American families living in big cities in the 1950s, his family lived in a middle-class section of Louisville, not in a poor ghetto. Still, Cash was full of resentment. He was a talented man, a fine painter of murals and a good singer, and he felt stifled in Southern society. Though he refused to leave his home state, he was sure that the white people of Louisville would never recognize his abilities. From time to time, when he grew mean with frustration, he would drink too much and stir up trouble for local police. In spite of Cash's occasional outbursts, Cassius Jr. and his younger brother Rudolph grew up in a relatively stable, happy environment. Odessa was a wonderful, caring mother, faithful to her Christian upbringing. She worked hard to instill the values of her Baptist faith in her children. As Cash remembered later, "My daddy used to say to me, 'Let them follow their mother because a woman is always better than a man.' So that's what I did, and their mother taught them right, taught them to believe in God and be spiritual and good to everybody."[1]

Cassius Jr. was a sweet, manageable boy. Little about him in those days suggested the outspoken fighter he was to become later. Odessa was surprised by her son's tendency to walk on his tiptoes, rather than flat-footed as most babies do.[2] But Cassius was not particularly enthusiastic about athletic competition as a young boy, preferring to shoot marbles or dodge stones that his brother Rudy would throw at him. He was more interested in testing his own agility than in competing against other kids in the neighborhood. That, of course, would soon change.

In October of 1954, Cassius rode his bicycle to the Louisville Home Show at Columbia Auditorium. The Home Show was a bazaar for African-American manufacturers and merchants in the Louisville area. After exploring the auditorium for a while, Cassius went back to the place where he left his bicycle and found that it had been stolen. In a fit of rage, he scoured the show, threatening to "whup" whoever had taken his bike. Finally, near tears, he wandered into the auditorium basement, where policeman Joe Martin was teaching some of the neighborhood boys to box. "Well," Martin said to Cassius, "you better learn to fight before you start challenging people that you're gonna whup."[3] For the first time, Cassius turned his attention to the boxing ring and slipped on the gloves.

Early on, Cassius displayed very little ability in the ring. He was an 89-pound (40.37-kg) twelve-year-old, a mere shadow of the near-perfect physical specimen he would soon become. But after six weeks of practice, he won a three-minute, three-round split decision against a neighborhood kid named Ronnie O'Keefe. The fight appeared on Joe Martin's local television boxing show, "To-

12

At age twelve, Cassius Clay was beginning his boxing career. Even then, his instructor noted, Cassius "always talked a good fight."

morrow's Champions." After the judges announced their decision, little Cassius shouted a claim that boxing fans would hear thousands of times over the next forty years: "I'll be the greatest fighter of all times!"[4] Once he tasted the glory of victory, and experienced the thrill of the spotlight, he was hooked.

In some ways, Cassius's decision to pursue boxing was fortunate, as it was a sport open to African-American athletes in 1954. Jackie Robinson had broken the baseball color barrier—the imaginary wall that kept African-Americans out of the major leagues—in 1947, but baseball, football, and basketball were still games dominated by white competitors. In contrast, boxing already had a long history of African-American challengers and champions, beginning with Peter Jackson in 1891. Following Jackson were a number of black champions in lighter weight classes. And then came Jack Johnson who, in 1908, won the heavyweight title, always the most important title in boxing. Fearful that a black champion would undermine the values of a segregated society and enrage white fans, boxing officials closed the door on African-American heavyweights after Johnson. It stayed closed until Joe Louis took the belt in 1937. Louis's dignified reign as champion won the hearts of blacks and whites alike, and opened boxing permanently to black challengers. By 1954 Cassius Clay's chosen sport was the most successfully integrated sport in America. Cassius took advantage of the situation. According to fellow boxer and Louisville pal Jimmy Ellis, "[Cassius] spent all his time in the gym. That's where he lived. He wanted to box and he wanted to be great, and that's what his life was all about."[5]

Being a champion, and especially a proud, worthy African-American champion, was important to Cassius early in his career. "When I was growing up," he would say many years later, "too many colored people thought it was better to be white. And I don't know what it was, but I always felt like I was born to do something for my people."[6] Most likely, the twelve-year-old Cassius was struggling just to stay in the ring and gave little thought to doing anything for his people. But with time he would come to understand the enormity of the African-American struggle for equality. Through boxing, he would find his own voice in that struggle.

Louisville was not as openly segregated as some of the cities in the Deep South, or as subtly discriminatory as some of the cities in the North. But Cassius and his brother understood that some places were off-limits to black people and that they would be called "niggers" from time to time by their neighbors. The highly publicized 1955 murder in Money, Mississippi, of Emmett Till, a black boy from Chicago, was Cassius's first hard lesson in race relations. Till, who was very close in age to the thirteen-year-old Cassius, had been bragging to some of his friends that he was dating a white girl. He said it loudly enough for some of the local whites to hear him. Later, acting on a dare, he said "Bye, baby," to a white woman in a store. Till disappeared shortly thereafter. He was later dragged from the Tallahatchie River, dead, with barbed wire wrapped around his neck. Cassius saw photographs of the boy's body in the newspapers, "his head swollen and bashed in, his eyes bulging out of their sockets and his mouth twisted and broken."[7] It was an image he would never forget.

By the late 1950s, civil rights tensions were reaching a boiling point. After African-Americans participated with honor in World War II and fought bravely in the Korean War, the U.S Army integrated its troops in 1951. Following the success of the military program, African-Americans demanded integration in other aspects of life in the United States. In 1954, the United States Supreme Court overturned an old federal policy (dating from 1896) that allowed the government to provide "separate but equal" educational facilities for children according to race. In the landmark case *Brown v. Board of Education*, the court decided that separate facilities were "inherently unequal" and that segregation in public buildings like schools was unconstitutional. Then, in 1955, Rosa Parks of Montgomery, Alabama, refused to give up her seat at the front of a city bus to please a white person and was arrested. In the protests that followed, 50,000 African-Americans boycotted the Birmingham buses, and a young minister named Martin Luther King, Jr., rose to national prominence. In 1957, President Dwight D. Eisenhower sent federal troops to Little Rock, Arkansas, to protect nine African-American children trying to enter a newly integrated high school.

These events served as a background for Cassius's childhood. He was a schoolboy when the age of protest began, and not a very good one at that. After attending Virginia Avenue Elementary School and DuValle Junior High School, he enrolled in Central High School in 1957. Disinterested and unsuccessful, he actually withdrew before the end of his first year, in March of 1958. Odessa persuaded him to try again the following year, and he stayed on to graduate in 1960. Out of a class of 391, he ranked 376, barely passing with a 72.7 average. Perhaps he spent too much time in the gym. More likely, he suffered from dyslexia, a learning impairment that affected his ability to read. Two of his own children would later be diagnosed as dyslexic.

As much as Cassius struggled in the classroom, and as little effort as he apparently put into his schoolwork, he worked hard in the gym, and was more successful in the ring at an early age than most boxers will ever be. By

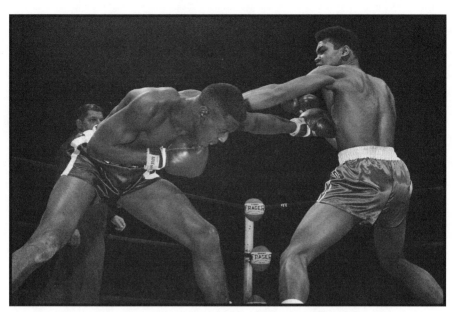

Cassius Clay taking on Jimmy Jones in a Golden Glove championship. Clay won on a judges' decision.

the time he reached his eighteenth birthday, he had fought 108 amateur bouts, won six Kentucky Golden Gloves competitions, two national Golden Gloves competitions, and two AAU titles. As an amateur, he had done it all . . . almost. The only challenge he had not faced was the international challenge, at the Olympic Games, and he had already earned a spot on the national team. As a boxer, he was ready. But as an inexperienced kid from Louisville, he was not so sure. The 1960 Olympic Games were held in Rome. Cassius had never been on a plane and he refused to fly now even with the promise of gold waiting on the other side of the ocean. Coach Joe Martin had a hard time convincing the United States' best 178-

pound (80.75-kg) fighter to get on the plane, but after much negotiation, Martin's good sense won the fighter over.

Once Cassius conquered his fear of flying and was safely in the air over the Atlantic, he proved to be the most magnetic figure on the United States team, perhaps the most likable athlete at the Games. His teammate and roommate in Rome, Wilbert "Skeeter" McClure, watched in awe as Cassius charmed the athletes and international media at Olympic Village: "He went around introducing himself and learning other people's names and swapping team lapel pins. If they'd had an election, he would have won in a walk," one teammate said.[8] And that's exactly how Cassius went through his competition in the ring: in a walk. He won two unanimous decisions and a second-round knockout before facing a tough Polish fighter, Zbigniew Pietrzykowski, in the gold medal match. Always concerned about putting on a good show for the crowd, Cassius wasted the first round mugging and showing off his quick feet. Late in the second round, he realized that if he continued his clowning, he would lose the match. So he turned up the heat in the final round and won the gold medal on points. In truth, Cassius had hardly been challenged in Rome. He was, quite simply, the best at the Games.

To the relief of boxing fans back home, the brash young fighter also proved that he could handle the responsibilities that came with Olympic gold. During this period, international athletic competition often reflected international political competition. With tensions between the Soviet Union and the United States at a high point in 1960, each gold medal won by one country was a blow to the other. In this spirit of political rivalry, a Soviet reporter asked Cassius what he thought of his native land. "U.S.A. is the best country in the world, in-

Clay (center) brought home the gold medal from the 1960 Olympic Games in Rome.

cluding yours," Cassius said. When the reporter reminded the boxer that the escalation of racial tensions in the United States could create problems for a black athlete, Cassius replied, "Tell your readers we got qualified people working on that, and I'm not worried about the outcome."[9] He was as quick with his tongue as he was with his feet.

And he was correct, there were "a lot of qualified people" working for the civil rights movement in 1960. In Greensboro, North Carolina, four students refused to leave their stools at a white lunch counter in a segregated restaurant. A rash of copycat "sit-ins" spread across the nation, proof that more and more people were heed-ing Martin Luther King, Jr.'s call for nonviolent, passive protest against racism. And, as if to disprove the beliefs underlying segregation, black athletes such as Wilma Rudolph–the first American woman to win three gold medals–and Cassius himself returned from the Rome Games as world champions and national heroes.

In later years, Cassius would claim that he had thrown his gold medal into the Ohio River when, home from the Olympics, he was turned out of a white restaurant in Louisville. "Threw it in the river," he would say. "Threw me out of a restaurant."[10] Occasionally he'd add a detail about being chased across the Ohio River by a white biker gang that demanded the medal as ransom.[11] Today, most of his friends believe that he made the stories up to illustrate the frustration and anger of African-Americans in the 1960s. In truth, he was warmly received when he returned from Rome. His first stop was New York City. Chaperoned by sportswriter Dick Schaap, Cassius visited the great Manhattan landmarks: boxer Jack Dempsey's restaurant, the famous Birdland jazz club, and Times Square. He was overjoyed when people on the streets recognized him, which was not too difficult since he was still wearing his Olympic jacket and gold medal. Then in Louisville, the celebration was even greater. He was driven by motorcade from the Louisville airport to a reception held in his honor. Central High School awarded him a letterman's jacket. The Kentucky legislature named him an honorary page. Cash even painted the steps of the family's house red, white, and blue.

In appreciation, Cassius recited a poem, the first of many, many boastful poems to come. He called it "How Cassius Took Rome":

To make America the greatest is my goal,
So I beat the Russian, and I beat the Pole,
And for the U.S.A. won the Medal of Gold.
Italians said, "You're greater than the Cassius of Old.
We like your name, we like your game.
So make Rome your home if you will."
I said, "I appreciate your kind hospitality,
But the U.S.A is my country still,
'Cause they waiting to welcome me in Louisville."[12]

2

The Louisville Lip

Boxers do not become champions overnight. They pound their bodies into shape. They survive grueling tests of endurance. They ignore injury and sickness. They are punched and shoved and pushed every day. And it all costs money. To be the best, a fighter needs to have a good staff of advisers and trainers—"cornermen"—and he needs good training equipment, the best heavy bags and speed bags and gloves and shoes. Since a fighter must train every day to become a champion, he cannot hold a regular job, and usually cannot pay his cornermen and buy his equipment without assistance. For Cassius

Clay, that assistance came in the form of the Louisville Sponsoring Group.

Louisville businessman Bill Faversham watched Cassius's progress through the Golden Gloves, the AAU circuit, and the Olympics. As vice president of a large corporation and a former investment counselor, Faversham knew a good investment when he saw one. Cassius had it all: talent, stunning good looks, and the kind of personality that could not be ignored. He was a celebrity in the making. So Faversham met with Cassius's family and convinced them that he was the best man to oversee Cassius's financial concerns. Faversham rounded up ten of his wealthy friends and convinced each to donate $2,800 to Cassius's training fund. Cassius received a $10,000 bonus for signing with the sponsoring group and a stipend of $333 a month, 15 percent of which was held in a pension fund until Cassius turned thirty-five or quit fighting. For taking a financial risk and supporting a boxer new to the professional ring, the eleven white entrepreneurs, now known as the Louisville Sponsoring Group, received half of Cassius's earnings for the first four years, and 40 percent after that. It was a reasonably fair arrangement that provided for Cassius's present needs as well as his future after boxing. But Cassius would soon become uncomfortable with the thought that eleven white men owned a piece of his success.

After the contract was settled, the group searched for a trainer, someone to help Cassius make the jump from the relatively simple world of amateur boxing to the brutal and often corrupt world of the pro fights. One of Cassius's early boxing idols, "Sugar" Ray Robinson, was still winding down his own career and refused to take on a protégé. Archie Moore, another active fighter, did not harbor such reservations and signed on as Cassius's trainer. Before heading out to Moore's camp at a salt mine in Ramona, California—35 miles (56 kilometers) outside San Diego—Cassius entered his first professional fight. On October 29, 1960, he made light work of a boxer named Tunney Hunsaker in Louisville, winning by decision after the scheduled six rounds. Then he was off to the West, to learn his trade in Moore's gym, a converted barn known as the "Bucket of Blood."

To Cassius's dismay, he learned more about buckets than blood during his short stay at Moore's camp. The older boxer believed in giving his outspoken apprentice a lesson in discipline before he began intensive training. Cassius, with a gold medal and a professional victory already under his belt, had to wash floors and clean dishes before he was allowed to enter a sparring session. As if that were not enough, Moore tried to correct Cassius's unconventional boxing technique. Cassius would have none of it. "I don't want to fight to be an old man," Cassius said when Moore tried to give him tips about survival in the ring. "That's all right for you, but I'm gonna only fight five or six years, make me two or three million dollars, and quit fighting."[1]

Coming from anyone else, these would have been idle promises. But Cassius had special abilities. Yes, his form was atrocious, exactly the kind of form that could get a young boxer injured. But as master trainer Eddie Futch explained later, "He had so much ability, he could always outrun his mistakes."[2] Instead of ducking punches, blocking them with his hands, and avoiding charging opponents, Cassius used his blindingly quick reflexes to avoid contact. He jerked his head backward fast enough to make other fighters miss him. He taunted opponents, keeping his hands down by his sides, exposing his chin for everyone to see, and then he took his chin away as his opponents' fists whizzed by. He did not simply beat other fighters, he frustrated them. Ferdie Pacheco, his longtime boxing physician, or "fight doctor," explained Cassius's success this way:

> *[Cassius] turned his faults into advantages. His great hand speed made it possible to hold his left at his waist. His leg speed made it possible to lean back, away from a punch. To hit [him] when he leaned back, you needed a stepladder and blinding speed. [He] gave you the body, and while you busily worked it, he pounded your head. . . . What else can you ask of a fighter? One thing is a mouth. Nonstop talking, bell to bell, to frustrate you, to wear you out, to confuse, befuddle, distract.*[3]

Yes, he was stubborn, arrogant, and vocal about wanting things his own way. But everyone could see his promise, his speed, his size, his charm, his smarts, and some probably even suspected what boxing historian Hank Kaplan would recognize years later: "Cassius Clay was the greatest innovator in the history of boxing."[4] With all of his technical weaknesses, perhaps *because* of his weaknesses, he would one day change the sport of boxing forever.

But he still had to get out of Moore's camp and find someplace better suited to his temperament and abilities. He returned to Louisville for the winter holidays in 1960, and he never went back to Ramona. In one of the luckiest breaks of Cassius's career, Faversham found Angelo Dundee, a respected trainer who, along with his brother Chris, owned the Fifth Street Gym in Miami. Angelo had met Cassius in 1957 during a trip to Louisville. At that time, Cassius, hearing that the famous Dundee brothers were in town, called their hotel room and asked to meet with them. Dundee agreed and the Clay boys, Cassius and Rudy, stayed in Dundee's hotel room for four hours talking about boxing. Dundee appreciated the kid's enthusiasm. Now, three years later, Dundee agreed to take on the young hotshot for $125 a week.

Cassius did not even wait for Christmas. As soon as he heard about an opening at Dundee's gym, the eighteen-year-old left his family again and headed for Miami. For the most part, Dundee was training Cuban boxers who had escaped the violence of Fidel Castro's 1956 communist rebellion. But he gave Cassius special attention, protected him from the rough crowd that frequented the gym, and from the prostitutes and gangsters who found lodging in the Mary Elizabeth Hotel, where Cassius was staying. Soon after arriving in Miami, Cassius won his second professional fight, beating Herb Siler, and then defeated Dundee's top contender, former world-champion Willie Pastrano, in a sparring round. And as Cassius continued to talk, boasting about his greatness as a fighter and his glorious future, more and more people started to notice him. They called him "The Louisville Lip" because of his incessant talking. He was loud and funny, and he drew crowds.

Dundee did a masterful job of bringing Cassius along: He organized fights with boxers who would challenge his young star without threatening his record. And Cassius did his job, too. In the first four months of 1961, he stomped through four opponents, allowing only one fight to extend past the third round. Dundee's training style, to "make the star feel that he's doing it on his own,"5 was working. At the same time, Cassius was learning important lessons from other fighters at Fifth Street. But Cassius was never afraid of the older, more experienced fighters, and he never backed down from any boxer, not even in a training session. When Ingemar Johansson came to Fifth Street to train for a title bout against heavyweight champion Floyd Patterson, Cassius

For many years, Cassius Clay boasted that he was ready to take on Floyd Patterson. This 1972 fight between the two men took place in New York.

volunteered to spar with him. He proceeded to beat the contender, dance around him, and mock him. "I'm the one who should be fighting Patterson, not you," he taunted as he slid around the ring. "Come on, here I am, come and get me, sucker."[6] After two embarrassing rounds in front of the Miami press, Johansson's manager pulled his fighter out of the ring and left Cassius to his dancing and his bragging.

As Cassius worked his way up the ranks, focusing on his future as a boxer, the civil rights movement entered a new era of activism. Black men and women, with the assistance of sympathetic whites, were organizing their own groups to join Martin Luther King, Jr.'s Southern Christian Leadership Conference in the fight for equality. The Congress of Racial Equality (CORE) and the Student Nonviolent Coordinating Committee (SNCC) were among the most powerful. Increasingly, these groups focused their attention not simply on the rural, segregated South, but also on the urban North.[7] Indeed, by 1961, it was clear that no section of the nation was free of racial tension. Cassius Clay, however, was still concentrating on his sport and on his climb to the top of the boxing world. Before he could make his own contribution to the profound and sweeping changes taking place in these years, he had to earn the nation's attention.

Few events were as important to Cassius's early celebrity as his chance meeting with the professional wrestler known as Gorgeous George. A flamboyant actor who wore his hair in long, golden locks and sprayed himself with perfume before entering the wrestling ring, George was a star because his act was outrageous. Some people loved him, and some hated him. But everyone watched him. In June of 1961, Cassius and Gorgeous George were invited to a dual interview by a Miami radio station. Cassius spoke first and tried his best to promote his upcoming fight with Duke Sabedong. Then it was George's turn to promote his upcoming wrestling matches. He put on quite a show. "I'll kill him," he screamed about his opponent. "I'll tear his arms off. If this bum beats me, I'll crawl across the ring and cut off my hair, but it's not gonna happen because I'm the greatest wrestler in the world."[8] Cassius realized immediately that Gorgeous George had the right formula for drawing a crowd.

Already a very good self-promoter, Cassius learned little things from Gorgeous George that helped him to perfect his act. He learned that making boxing fans angry was just as good as making them happy; either way, they would come to see him fight. He learned that white shoes and trunks made him look faster. And he learned that daring and risk-taking were just as important in fight promotion as they were in the ring. His gimmick for the next batch of fights was simple: He predicted the round in which he'd knock out his opponent. In the late summer and fall of 1961, Cassius fought three fights televised on ABC's "Gillette Cavalcade of Sports." The first two were humdrum affairs, both Clay victories, but Cassius had something special planned for the third, against Willie Besmanoff: "I'm embarrassed to get into the ring with this unrated duck. I'm ready for top contenders like Patterson and Sonny Liston. Besmanoff must fall in seven."[9] In truth, Besmanoff probably would not have lasted seven rounds if Cassius boxed hard from the opening bell. As Dundee screamed at his fighter to "stop playing," Cassius danced around the ring, mugged for the crowd, and did everything he could to postpone the knockout until the seventh round. Next came Sonny Banks, who succeeded in knocking down Cassius for the first time in his professional career. But Cassius recovered quickly enough to knock out Banks in the predicted fourth round. Against Don Warner, Cassius miscalculated. He knocked Warner out a round too early. After the fight, Cassius announced that Warner had refused to shake hands before the fight, so he subtracted one round for poor sportsmanship. As television audiences watched this unbelievable fighter make his predictions come true, Cassius kept repeating what he had been saying for years: "I am the greatest of all times!" By 1962, it was clear that Cassius had learned everything Gorgeous George had to teach, and then some.

In 1962, boxing needed the lighthearted spark that Cassius provided. That year, two tragedies renewed the public's recurring fear that boxing was too brutal to be sanctioned by the government. First, in March, welterweight Emile Griffith punched Benny "Kid" Paret to death in the ring. A short time later, featherweight Sugar Ramos beat Davey Moore so badly that Moore died of his injuries after the fight. In addition, fight promoter Frankie Carbo was imprisoned for activities related to organized crime. The International Boxing Club, which governed a large portion of the nation's fights, was disbanded for similar reasons. After holding a virtual monopoly on televised boxing, ABC discontinued its Gillette series in response to the public outcry against the vicious, corrupt sport. But then came Cassius Clay. For better or worse, his looks, humor, and talent saved the sport during this difficult period.

On November 15, 1962, almost two years after he left Archie Moore's camp to try his luck with Dundee, Cassius had the chance to test his skills against his former teacher. Moore had fallen on difficult financial times and needed a big fight to replenish his bank account. Cassius needed the experience and wanted bragging rights. He wanted to prove to his first professional trainer, and to the rest of the boxing world, that he was ready for the big time. Of course he threw his first flurry of jabs with his tongue. Moore had always been a good talker, but he was outclassed this time. "Archie's been living off the fat of the land," Cassius shouted in his now-familiar poetic rhythm. "I'm here to give him his pension plan./ When you come to the fight, don't block the aisle and don't block the door./ You will all go home after round four."[10] More than 16,200 fans paid a record total of $182,000 to see Cassius make good on his promise. And he did. Moore was down in four.

A few months later, he knocked out Charlie Powell in the third round as predicted. Then came Doug Jones at Madison Square Garden. Cassius was always a little tight before matches in the Garden, boxing's legendary capital. Rejecting the advice of his trainer and handlers, he arrived at the arena two and a half hours before the fight began. He worked out the whole time, skipping rope and punching bags to calm himself down. By the time the bell rang to start the fight, he was slow and tired. The fight went the distance, ten rounds, and not the four that Cassius had predicted. He won the decision, but some boxing experts argued that the judges were more lenient in their scoring because Cassius was becoming a superstar. They argued that his reputation and not his performance had won the fight. Cassius would hear this accusation from time to time as his career progressed.

As he became more famous, Cassius surrounded himself with an entourage of people dedicated to serving him. This entourage, later called the "Ali Circus," was a varied assortment of characters. On one hand, there were devoted companions such as Howard Bingham, a photographer for *Life* magazine, *Sports Illustrated*, and other periodicals. Cassius met Bingham in 1962, and the two have been nearly inseparable ever since. On the other hand, there were strange, needy characters such as Drew

Drew "Bundini" Brown was part of the entourage known as the "Ali Circus."

"Bundini" Brown, men who were down on their luck and needed work as well as companionship. At age thirteen, Bundini had been a U.S. Navy messboy, was discharged at fifteen for attacking an officer with a meat cleaver, traveled the globe as a merchant marine, and even worked for Sugar Ray Robinson for a short time. By the time he met up with Cassius, before the Jones fight, he was an occasional drunk and an incredibly entertaining companion and roommate for Cassius on the road. Bundini's nonsensical cheers, his incessant "Stick 'em champ," soon became as familiar to boxing fans as Cassius's white shoes and flashy footwork. Over the years, the entourage would grow in proportion to Cassius's fame. But the fighter seldom turned these men away. Even the outrageous Bundini, who would later steal Cassius's heavyweight belt and pawn it for cash, was always welcomed back to the camp in the end.[11] Cassius understood that, as a champion, he could help these people achieve something meaningful and give shape to their lives. Besides, he liked the attention that the large entourage showered on him.

By the summer of 1963, Cassius was a proven winner, undefeated with an 18–0 record. In June, he invaded the British Isles for a fight at Wembley Stadium outside of London. His opponent was the top British contender, Henry Cooper, who was known as a good puncher but a "bleeder"—a fighter who cut and bled easily. Since a severe cut is grounds for disqualification, Cooper's weakness was a serious disadvantage. To the dismay of British fans, Cassius promised a fifth-round knockout. In front of 55,000 British fans, he entered the ring in Wembley, wearing royal robes and a crown, mocking the British royal family; emblazoned on the back of the robe were the words "Cassius the Greatest." Cooper turned out to be less trouble than anyone expected. By round four,

Cassius was practically holding him up, waiting for the fifth round before he delivered, once again, on his prediction. But then the unthinkable happened: Cooper gathered the strength for a final left hook and connected, sending a shocked and now hurt Cassius Clay through the ropes. The referee had already counted to four when the bell sounded to end the round. According to British rules, the referee had to stop counting. Cassius was literally saved by the bell. Then he was saved by his trainer. Dundee, who had noticed a tear in Cassius's glove earlier in the match, decided to make the tear worse. He called the glove to the referee's attention. Fearing that a torn glove could be dangerous to a bleeder like Cooper, the referee directed Cassius's cornermen to put a new glove on him. While Cooper waited, Cassius got a massage and some smelling salts to wake him up. By the time the fifth round started, he had recovered from the knockdown. By the end of the round, he had beaten Cooper so badly, and Cooper was bleeding so much, that the referee stopped the fight. Cassius was certainly a great fighter, but this time he was lucky that Dundee was a great cornerman.

By the end of 1963, Cassius Clay was becoming a household name, and a major sports celebrity. And his fame was stretching beyond the ring. Capitalizing on his success, Columbia Records asked Cassius to record some of his poems for a new album. Among the more memorable lyrics was the boast, "It's hard to be modest when you're as great as I am."[12] And he wasn't even champion yet. The belt would come soon enough. But first Cassius had to confront important issues about his place as a black athlete in an increasingly divided society.

3
A
Champion

In winning the presidential election of 1960, John F. Kennedy ushered in a new era in national politics. Adored by the public and the press alike, the young, handsome president was perceived as a champion of youth and progress. For the first two years of his administration, however, Kennedy ignored one of the most important issues of the era, the civil rights movement. Early in the decade, black and white students began a national campaign known as the "Freedom Rides" to desegregate bus depots. Black students fought to enroll in whites-only universities such as the University of Mississippi. And protests in the South grew violent as white police officers in Birmingham, Alabama, turned powerful fire hoses on civil rights demonstrators. A frightened nation watched these proceedings each night on television news programs. In his third year as president, Kennedy finally made the struggle for equality a part of his administration's agenda. "A great change is at hand," he declared during a television speech, "and our task, our obligation, is to make that revolution, that change, peaceful and constructive for all."[1] Kennedy's new plan was to generate support for integration and for a new federal bill prohibiting discrimination in government programs. In a show of support for the president's proposed bill, Martin Luther King, Jr., and the civil rights leadership organized a march on Washington, D.C. The march culminated in King's famous "I Have a Dream" speech on the steps of the Lincoln Memorial. For this speech, and for years of courageous work around the country, King won the Nobel Peace Prize in 1964.

What King realized, perhaps better than any other civil rights leader, was that television could be used as a tool in the struggle. In the 1960s, over 90 percent of all American households owned at least one television set.[2] King's nonviolent protests were designed to create stark images of good versus evil for these growing television audiences. Using the television cameras as allies, King proved to the nation that its treatment of African-Americans was intolerable.

And as television became a major force in American culture, Cassius Clay rose to prominence. With his handsome face, his near-perfect athlete's body, his obvious talent as a boxer, and his now-famous mouth, Cassius was a made-for-TV hero. And television gave him influence. Everywhere he turned, a camera was directed at him, sending his image across the country and around the world. Suddenly, whatever he said and did had consequences. People, particularly black people, looked to him as a role model. Courageously, the twenty-one-year-old boxer accepted the responsibility and began speaking his mind.

Cassius watched scenes of racially motivated violence on television and, like so many others, was disgusted by what he saw. He understood that, through boxing, he had been granted privileges other African-Americans could only dream about. "Where do you think I'd be next week if I didn't know how to shout and holler and make the public take notice?" he would ask. "I'd be poor and I'd probably be down in my home town, washing windows or running an elevator and saying 'yes suh' and 'no suh' and knowing my place."[3] Like his hero, boxer Jack Johnson, Cassius was not about to play by any of the old rules.

Jack Johnson had lived a reckless life. When in 1908 he became the first black heavyweight champion, white boxing fans panicked. The heavyweight champion had always been a symbol of athletic superiority, an ambassador of the sport. To boxing officials, a black champion suggested that white men were no longer good fighters. And Johnson did little to ease their concerns. He bragged about his title and his talent in the ring. When Johnson married a white woman in 1913, boxing officials finally reached the limit of their patience. The Bureau of Investigation (later the FBI) decided that his interracial marriage was illegal under the laws of the times and Johnson was sentenced to a year in jail and a $1,000 fine. He escaped his jail term by running to Canada, and then to England. In 1915, after losing a bout against "white hope" Jess Willard, Johnson returned to the States and lived in relative peace until he died in 1946. To the African-Americans of his age, Jack Johnson represented a new kind of "Negro," one who refused to accept the prejudices of his white countrymen and his secondary status under United States law.[4]

By 1963, Cassius was on his way to becoming the Jack Johnson of his own era. But instead of marrying white women and stirring up trouble during alcoholic fits, as Johnson had done, Cassius became an important figure in the civil rights movement by voicing his religious and political opinions. For three years, Cassius secretly attended meetings of a religious group known as the Nation of Islam. Following the teachings of their two most important ministers, founder Elijah Muhammad and Malcolm X, and under the influence of the Nation's Miami agent, "Captain" Sam Saxon (also known as Abdul Rahaman), Cassius was now considering a complete conversion.

The Nation of Islam combined the teachings of the orthodox Islamic faith with the teachings of the black nationalist movement. The followers of orthodox Islam, known as Muslims, believe in the teachings of the prophet Muhammad, who was born in A.D. 570 and received revelations from the angel Gabriel, which were then written down in a holy book known as the Qur'an. The Nation of Islam accepted Muhammad's teachings but added its own twist to the Islamic tradition. In the Nation's version, the world began with black people in the city of Mecca, in present-day Saudi Arabia. These people formed a tribe known as Shabazz. About 6,600 years ago, a Shabazz scientist known as Yacub was banished from Mecca for his evil teachings. Yacub, in revenge for his banishment, created a race of devils with white skin to terrorize the black-skinned Shabazz. Then the Nation's story skips ahead to the summer of 1930, when a silk salesman known as Wallace D. Fard (later known as Farrad Muhammad) arrived in Detroit. There Fard met a man named Elijah Poole. Fard described to Poole the story of the tribe of Shabazz and claimed to be Allah in human form. In 1934, Fard disappeared, leaving Elijah as his messenger. Poole accepted a new Muslim name, Elijah Muhammad, and organized a new religion from his home in Detroit. The religion spread through black communities. From orthodox Islam, Elijah adopted the rules for behavior: dietary laws, rules about modesty in speech and dress, limits on relationships between men and women. Elijah directed his new teachings at underprivileged black people in urban ghettos. He tried to give his listeners confidence in themselves and in their fellow members of the Nation of Islam. But perhaps his most popular teachings were about the evils that "white devils" had perpetrated against blacks throughout history. Instead of integration and reconciliation, Elijah preached division. Because of his speeches, the U.S. government and a majority of white people in the country viewed him with skepticism and even fear.

Even more successful at converting African-Americans to the Nation of Islam was Elijah's fiery deputy, Malcolm X. Born Malcolm Little in Omaha, Nebraska, Malcolm dropped his last name, his "slave name," after he converted in the late 1940s. Once a well-known criminal operating along the eastern seaboard of the United States, Malcolm received letters from Elijah while he was in prison in 1948. Upon his release, Malcolm worked for the Nation, spreading Elijah's word and opening new temples in cities throughout the country. As a reward, Elijah allowed Malcolm to open a temple in New York City's Harlem, once the site of Malcolm's most disturbing crimes. He soon became the most popular speaker in the Nation and a national figure. His was the violent, radical alternative to Martin Luther King, Jr.'s more peaceful, integrationist brand of civil rights.

Cassius was ripe for conversion to the Nation in 1963. He remembered the murder of Emmett Till. He had seen the violence between whites and blacks on television. It certainly did not look like white people were willing to desegregate peacefully or treat African-Americans fairly once they had desegregated. Only the Nation of Islam encouraged Cassius to believe that he was every

*Cassius Clay signing autographs in New York,
accompanied by Muslim leader Malcolm X
(at left, with hat and glasses)*

person's equal. By the fall of 1963, newspapers were starting to report Cassius's presence at Nation of Islam rallies, calling the Nation "the Black Muslims." On January 21, 1964, *The New York Herald* reported that Cassius had spoken at a Nation meeting and was traveling with Malcolm X. "[U]nquestionably," the reporter wrote, "he sympathizes with Muslim aims and by his presence at their meetings lends them prestige. He is the first nationally famous Negro to take an active part in the Muslim movement."[5] Cassius's brother Rudy had officially joined the Nation first. It was only a matter of time before Cassius followed.

In the meantime, Cassius was on a different quest: to find Sonny Liston, the heavyweight champion of the world, and frustrate Liston into giving him a shot at the title. Though he was fighting well and was still undefeated, Cassius was not yet Liston's top contender and should not have gotten a title fight. But he was tired of waiting and knew that if he could make himself enough of a nuisance, Liston would give in and fight him. So he announced to the press that he, Bundini, and Bingham were going to haunt Liston until the champion was angry enough to sign a fight contract.

The trio traveled to Las Vegas and taunted Liston while he was trying to entertain himself at the casinos. They mocked Liston to television reporters. Worst of all, but most successful of all, they drove to Liston's house in Denver. When the press arrived, Cassius was wearing a denim jacket that said "Bear Huntin' " across the back, called Liston a "big, ugly bear," and set a bear trap on Liston's lawn. It was a brilliant bit of fight promotion. Not even Gorgeous George had gone this far. On November 5, 1963, Liston signed the fight contract. The title bout was scheduled for February 25, 1964, in Miami Beach.

Liston was a 6–1 favorite in the match. Some people were jokingly offering 3–1 odds that Liston would kill Cassius. Not even the Louisville Sponsoring Group thought the fight with Liston was a good idea. Charles "Sonny" Liston was the most feared man in boxing. He had learned to box in prison while serving time for armed robbery. He climbed to the top of the professional ranks in impressive fashion, knocking out almost everyone he faced. At 6 feet 1 inch (1.85 m) and 210 pounds (95.25 kg), he was physically imposing. Known for his angry scowl, his heavy punches, and his connections to organized crime, Liston seemed downright mean. No one had ever challenged him as brazenly as Cassius was challenging him now. "I'm young and handsome and fast and pretty and can't possibly be beat," Cassius shouted during his training sessions.[6] He repeatedly called Liston the "big, ugly bear," joked with the press, and showed no sign of fear. "I'm going to put that ugly bear on the floor," he told reporters, "and after the fight I'm gonna build myself a pretty home and use him as a bear skin rug. Liston even smells like a bear." Liston issued an ominous reply: "I might hurt that boy bad."[7]

The Fifth Street Gym was packed each day Cassius trained. Spectators paid fifty cents apiece to watch the Cassius Clay circus in action. Even the Beatles, the British rock band, paid him a visit. But there were problems in Cassius's camp. Following the assassination of President Kennedy on November 22, 1963, Malcolm X delivered insensitive remarks to the press about Kennedy's responsibility for the increasing violence among white people in the United States. His comments provoked a public outcry. Elijah Muhammad, jealous of the media attention Malcolm had been receiving, used the controversy to his favor and suspended his rival from the Nation's temples for ninety days. Cassius, still loyal to his friend, invited Malcolm to stay in Miami for the fight. But Elijah had already sent one of his eight children, Herbert, to Cassius's camp to make sure that the fighter did not stray from the Nation's teachings. With both sides of the feuding Nation in Cassius's camp, tensions ran high. Malcolm tried his best to shield Cassius from the controversy, however, and became the fighter's spiritual advisor: "Do you think Allah has brought about all this intending for you to leave the ring as anything but the champion?"[8]

As Cassius balanced his responsibilities to the Nation with his training, Liston remained calm, even too calm. "I don't know what I'm training so hard for—this kid ain't gonna last one round," he boasted.[9] Boxing experts agreed. But Cassius had a surprise in store for everyone. On the morning of the fight, when Cassius arrived at the weigh-in, former champion Sugar Ray Robinson stood at his side, advising him to remain calm. But the moment Liston arrived, escorted by Joe Louis, the weigh-in press conference collapsed in confusion. As Bundini chanted, "Float like a butterfly, sting like a bee. Rumble, young man. Rumble," Cassius attacked Liston like an insane man, screaming, "I got you now, Sonny. I got your championship now!"[10] Six people restrained Cassius as he challenged the heavyweight champion. The chairman of the Miami Boxing Commission fined him $2,500 on the spot. The fight was almost postponed because Cassius had driven his blood pressure up to a dangerous level during the outburst. When Dr. Ferdie Pacheco asked Cassius why he had behaved so poorly, Cassius replied, "Because Liston is a bully, and a bully is scared of a crazy man. . . . Now Liston thinks I'm crazy. I got him worried."[11] When he finally calmed down enough to weigh in, he registered at 210 pounds (95.25 kg), while the shorter Liston tipped the scales at 218 (98.88 kg). Slowly but surely, the momentum was swinging in Cassius's favor.

Cassius prepared for his own fight by watching from a back aisle as his brother fought his first professional match. He shouted instructions and gloated as Rudy won the first fight of his short career. But it was not yet time to celebrate. When Rudy stepped out of the ring, Cassius put him in charge of his water bottle, fearing that Liston's friends in organized crime would try to poison him. And his fear of Liston stayed with him for the first few rounds of the fight. He won the first round by jabbing at Liston's face and using his footspeed to avoid Liston's retaliations, but he lost the second round when he tried to out-box Liston using Liston's own style—hands up,

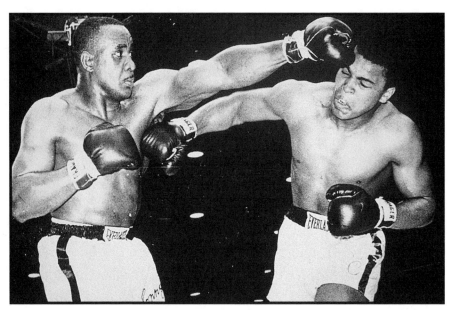

Clay matched up against Sonny Liston in Miami, 1964.

calm, quiet. Learning his lesson, he came back in the
third and fourth doing what he did best—dancing, jabbing, taunting his opponent. By the end of round four,
Liston was cut and bleeding, but something was wrong
with Cassius too. His left eye was red and swollen, and
he was complaining that he could not see. He begged
Dundee to cut his gloves off between rounds four and
five, ready to quit the match. By accident, or perhaps
on purpose, the liniment Liston's cornermen used on his
cut had gotten into Cassius's eyes. The young fighter
was sure he could not go on, but Dundee would not let
him think about quitting, especially when he was so
close to the belt. "This is for the heavyweight champi-

onship; no one walks away from that," the trainer said. "Get in there and run until your eyes clear up."[12] So Cassius avoided Liston for almost all of round five, until his eyes cleared, as Dundee said they would. Then he was talking and punching and dancing again. And it was more of the same in round six.

At the end of round six, Liston was complaining about a painful, stiff shoulder. He refused to stand up as the bell sounded for round seven. The fight was over, and Cassius Clay was heavyweight champion of the world. He whooped and shouted and lurched across the ring in excitement. When sportscaster Howard Cosell shoved his way up to Cassius for a post-fight interview, the new champion was almost incoherent: "I must be the greatest. I showed the world! I talk to God every day! I shook up the world! I'm the king of the world! I'm pretty! I'm a bad man!"[13] In contrast to Liston, who had a criminal record and was simply too frightening to be a popular champion, boxing now had a potential superstar in the top slot.

But the celebration did not last long. Cassius Clay refused to be the kind of champion the boxing establishment had dreamed about. During the press conference the morning after the fight, he announced to the world that he had converted from Christianity to Islam and that he was a follower of Elijah Muhammad. "I know where I'm going and I know the truth and I don't have to be what you want me to be," he said.[14]

The next morning he elaborated on his decision: "I'm the heavyweight champion, but right now there are some neighborhoods I can't move into. . . . I'm not joining no forced integration movement because it don't work. A man has got to know where he belongs."[15] Within months, Congress, under the direction of the new president, Lyndon B. Johnson, would pass the bill that

Kennedy had been fighting for before his assassination: the Civil Rights Act of 1964 barring discrimination in areas of public accommodation (theaters, restaurants, libraries, hospitals, etc.). But for Cassius and the Nation of Islam, it was too little, too late.

Perhaps the most shocking announcement in the days following the Liston fight was that Cassius Clay would change his name. "I have always been proud of my name," he had said years earlier.[16] But his opinion had changed after he heard Elijah Muhammad speak. Now, no matter how honorable the old abolitionist ambassador had been in an earlier century, and no matter how proud Cassius had been of his namesake in previous years, he was calling Cassius Clay his "slave name," a name that symbolized white oppression. So he abandoned his last name and adopted the Nation of Islam's replacement, "X," until he could be given a holy name by Elijah Muhammad.

By announcing his conversion so soon after his championship fight, Cassius gave up instant celebrity for instant notoriety. Certainly white boxing fans rejected his views, and the "white devil" views of the Nation, as racist and dangerous to the fragile peace of the United States in the mid-1960s. But black athletes like Floyd Patterson and Jackie Robinson turned their backs on Cassius as well. Even Cassius's parents were angry and hurt by the announcement. Cash Clay, in his typically fiery style, sounded a call to arms against the Nation: "They have ruined my two boys. They should run those Black Muslims out of the country before they ruin other fine people."[17]

On March 6, 1964, Elijah Muhammad made the announcement that Cassius had been waiting for. Cassius X was now to be known throughout the world as Muhammad Ali. The name means "most high," but when it was bestowed on Cassius Clay, it brought nothing but jeers and anger. It would be ten years before the name truly gained acceptance in the United States. For the first time in his life, Cassius Clay was booed.

4

Ali

If Cassius Clay was a national hero during the 1960 Olympics and the pride of Louisville during his climb to the top of the boxing world, Muhammad Ali was a national outcast after his conversion announcement. With the end of his popularity at home, Ali took his show abroad, to meet his fans in Africa. On May 14, 1964, Ali set out with Bingham, Herbert Muhammad, and Rudy— now called Rahaman Ali—to conquer what he considered his ancestral land. Few athletes from the United States had ever given much thought to their fans abroad, but Ali was prepared now to reach across the globe, particularly to poor, underdeveloped nations. He wanted to legitimize his title as heavyweight champion of the *world*.

The party's first stop was Ghana, where Ali was met by President Kwame Nkrumah and greeted as a hero for taking on the U.S. government and its discriminatory policies. On the next stop, in Nigeria, the reception was

During his trip to West Africa, Ali made this stop in Nigeria. "Who's the king?" he asked the children. "You're the king," they replied.

less enthusiastic, so Ali continued on to Egypt, an Islamic country. The Egyptians were even happier to greet him than the Ghanaians had been. He was a curiosity, a Muslim from the States. And, as Malcolm X had predicted, he was now seen as a living embodiment of Allah's power. He had challenged Sonny Liston, and all of Christian America, and had won both fights.

Meanwhile, Malcolm X was also in Africa, touring after his first pilgrimage to Mecca. In addition to the wonderful, eye-opening events of the pilgrimage, including his own conversion to orthodox Islam, Malcolm witnessed the first seeds of the Ali legend spreading through the Muslim world. Whenever he announced that he was from the United States, someone would ask him if he was the great Muhammad Ali. According to Malcolm, word of Ali's accomplishments had traveled faster than anyone could have imagined:

> *"I was later to learn that apparently every man, woman and child in the Muslim world had heard how Sonny Liston (who in the Muslim world had the image of a man-eating ogre) had been beaten in Goliath-David fashion by Cassius Clay, who then had told the world that his name was Muhammad Ali and his religion was Islam and Allah had given him his victory."*[1]

In Ghana, Malcolm and Ali actually crossed paths. Months earlier it would have been a joyful occasion. But after the Liston fight, Elijah banished Malcolm from the Nation, and Ali supported Elijah's decision. He was no longer allowed to associate with his old friend. Their first, chance meeting in Ghana was awkward, and Ali walked away before Malcolm had a chance to speak. When they met a second time, both mumbled only a few simple words.

50

Malcolm's philosophy changed considerably during his travels in the Middle East and Africa. In Mecca, he learned that the orthodox Islamic faith had nothing to do with the story of W. D. Fard, the tribe of Shabazz, or the scientist Yacub. And when he observed white people in mosques praying to Allah alongside black Muslims, he decided to rethink his ideas about racial problems in the United States. The man who once called white people the "enemy" who created "pure *hell* on this earth" for black people, was changing his views.[2] "The true Islam," he announced, "has shown me that a blanket indictment of all white people is as wrong as when whites make blanket indictments against blacks."[3]

But, no matter how much his opinions had changed, Malcolm was trapped by his past. The people of the United States continued to see him as a figure of racial division, and Ali continued to see him as a traitor to Elijah Muhammad. Malcolm was hurt when Ali ignored him in Africa but understood the pressures mounting on the young champion, the new spokesman for the Nation. "I felt like a blood big-brother to him," Malcolm said. "I'm not against him. He's a fine young man. Smart. He's just let himself be used, led astray."[4]

Upon his return from Africa, Ali experienced another major change in his life: He fell in love. In early July 1964, Herbert Muhammad introduced Ali to Sonji Roi, a beautiful twenty-three-year-old cocktail waitress who already had a three-year-old son from a previous relationship. Sonji may not have been a boxing champion, but she had a much better understanding of the world than the younger Ali. She traveled with a faster crowd than the straight, serious men of the Nation of Islam. Against the Clays' objections, and the objections of the Nation, Ali and Sonji were married a month after their first meeting. But the marriage never really had a chance to succeed. The Nation put too many restrictions on Sonji's lifestyle, and Ali was too loyal to Elijah Muhammad to compromise his faith for the sake of his new bride. And, with his rematch against Sonny Liston scheduled for November 16 in Boston, his attention was turning back to the ring.

As was his habit, Ali fattened up on cake and cookies after the first Liston fight and had to lose twenty pounds (nine kg) to be at his optimal weight for the second fight. It is possible that he trained too hard. Three days before the fight, at his training camp in Lewiston, Maine, he collapsed from severe abdominal pain. He was immediately rushed to a local hospital. Doctors discovered that he had an inguinal hernia, a tear in his abdominal wall. They performed emergency surgery, and the Liston fight was postponed.

On February 21, 1965, Malcolm X was assassinated in Harlem by an unidentified gunman. Many people suspect that the assassin was a fanatical follower of Elijah Muhammad. In time, Ali came to regret the way he and the rest of the Nation had treated Malcolm, particularly since Ali himself would come to the same conclusions that Malcolm had come to in Mecca: "It was a pity and a disgrace he died like that, because what Malcolm saw was right, and after he left us, we went his way anyway. Color didn't make a man a devil. It's the heart, soul and mind that counts."[5] Never a particularly vocal supporter of the "white devil" theory to begin with (he continued to seek the advice of white cornermen Dundee and Pacheco), Ali nevertheless would take several more years to announce that he too had turned away from the fundamental teachings of Elijah Muhammad.

Following the banishment and then the murder of Malcolm X, Elijah Muhammad changed the focus of the Nation's teachings. The physical separation of the races was no longer a top priority. Now Elijah's main goal was to foster self-sufficiency within the Nation. He criticized the dependency of African-Americans on stores owned by white proprietors, and he encouraged the construction of stores and restaurants to be operated by Muslims for a specifically Muslim clientele. Because the new message was about the economic survival of blacks in the United States, Ali was never asked to speak in the inflammatory style that Malcolm had mastered.

Two days after the assassination, the Nation's New York headquarters was bombed by Malcolm's supporters. Fearing that the violence would spread to Ali's fights, and claiming that the Liston rematch was organized by members of criminal organizations, Massachusetts boxing authorities withdrew their offer to host the Ali-Liston match. The fight's promoters finally settled on a small youth center in Lewiston, Maine, St. Dominic's Arena, as the site of the long-awaited rematch, scheduled for May 25, 1965.

It was a frightening training period for both fighters. Liston feared that agents of the Nation would hurt him before the fight, and Ali was receiving death threats from Liston's friends in organized crime and from the white supremacist Ku Klux Klan. The governor of Maine sent extra security guards to Ali's camp, to supplement the Muslim guards, the Fruit of Islam, already stationed there. Two guards were also assigned to Liston. No one was comfortable.

Finally, on May 25, the wait was over. A little more than four thousand people showed up in Lewiston to see an unpopular new champion fight an unpopular former champion in the middle of the Maine woods. The bell rang, the fighters met at center ring, and as the crowd was settling into its seats, Liston hit the canvas. He had thrown a jab that missed, and Ali countered with a short

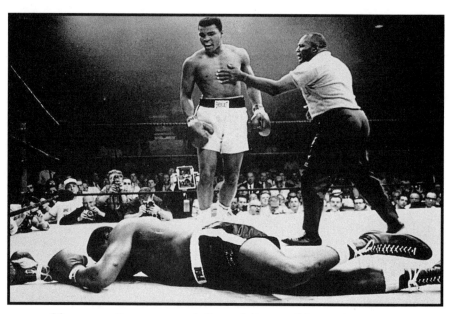

Clay standing over a defeated Sonny Liston in Lewiston, Maine

right to the side of his head. It would be forever known as the "Phantom Punch" for its ghostly strength. No one believed the punch was hard enough to knock out the mean ex-champion, not even Ali who shouted, "Get up, you bum! No one is going to believe this!"[6] Ex-champion Jersey Joe Walcott, the celebrity referee, had a hard time ushering Ali to a neutral corner so his count was delayed. By the time he ushered Ali away, Liston's head cleared and he was standing again. But before Walcott could resume the fight, Nat Fleischer, publisher of *Ring* boxing magazine, walked down to the ring from the audience, attracted Walcott's attention, and announced that Liston had already been down for seventeen seconds and that he should be counted out. Walcott had been an excellent fighter, but he was not a good referee. He listened to Fleischer's claims, agreed with them, and ended the fight, scoring it a first-round knockout. It was a dismal climax to the Ali-Liston rivalry. But Ali promoted the fight to the very end. Watching a replay of the knockdown after the fight, he joked, "I'm so fast, even I missed the punch."[7]

Many people still believe that Liston lost the fight on purpose. Some say he feared retaliation from the Nation of Islam if he defeated Ali. Others say he lost the fight to cover the bets of his mobster friends. But years later, testifying before the California Boxing Commission while applying for his state boxing license, he explained the "Phantom Punch" incident in a way that reminded his listeners of Ali's antics before the first fight:

> *Commissioner, Muhammad Ali is a crazy man. You can't tell what a crazy man is going to do. He was standing over me, Jersey Joe couldn't control him, and if I got up, I got to put one glove on the canvas to push myself up, and as soon as my knees clears the canvas Ali is going to be beating on me. The man is crazy, and I figured I ain't getting up till someone controls him.*[8]

As Ali predicted, the bully was scared of the crazy man. Before they ever entered the ring together, Ali had conquered Liston's mind.

Despite the controversy surrounding his second victory over Liston, Ali had backed up his claims—he was without question the best boxer of the age. Outside of the ring, however, Muhammad Ali was troubled. In

June, he and Sonji separated. Her inability to follow the very strict rules of the Nation of Islam were at the heart of their problems. By January 1966, they were officially divorced. Ali's alimony payments were set at $15,000 a year for ten years. While he was wrapped up in his divorce proceedings, Ali was also forced by the Nation to separate himself from Bundini. Elijah Muhammad objected to Bundini's sporadic drinking spells, his carelessness with money, and, reminiscent of Jack Johnson, his interest in white women. He was banished from Ali's camp for five years. But the worst blow of all was the Nation's role in separating Ali from his parents. By late 1965, tensions within the Clay family had reached a new level. Odessa attributed these tensions to Ali's handlers, their distrust for people outside of the Nation, and their peculiar ideas about race and skin color: "He's been told to stay away from his father because of the religious thing, and I imagine they've told him to stay away from me too. Muslims don't like me because I'm too fair-complected."[9]

In November, just as his life was slipping out of control, Ali defended his title against Floyd Patterson, the champion who preceded Sonny Liston. Patterson unwisely decided to make the fight a kind of religious war. Refusing to use Ali's Muslim name, he criticized the Nation and their views toward white people: "No decent person can look up to a champion whose credo is 'hate whites.'. . . Cassius Clay must be beaten and the Black Muslim scourge removed from boxing."[10]

Nothing Patterson could have said would have upset Ali as much as this attack on the Nation of Islam. He called the African-American Patterson an "Uncle Tom," a black man who caters to the demands of white people. In truth, Ali never pushed the "hate whites" aspect of the Nation of Islam's teachings. Most of Ali's statements revolved around the idea of African-American pride:

> *When I was growing up, what did I see? Jesus is white. Superman is white. The presidents is white. The angels is white. Santa Claus is white. That's brainwashing, the biggest lie ever told children. Every year, you buy toys, and your children wind up thinking they come from some white man with rosy cheeks. They think everything good has to come from someone white.* [11]

This part of Ali's message was positive. After centuries of discrimination, African-Americans had to regain self-confidence, to believe that "everything good" could just as easily come from black people as white people. But in 1965, Ali was an easy target for the kind of criticisms Patterson was offering. He would continue to be a target until he publicly rejected the Nation's "white devil" theories.

Patterson paid for his accusations. On November 22, in Las Vegas, Ali toyed with the aging ex-champion for twelve rounds, hurting Patterson but refusing to knock him out. Dundee begged Ali to end the fight, but the fighter refused.[12] He punished Patterson for all of the complications that had arisen in his life since the first Liston fight. The referee stopped the slaughter in round twelve. After the fight, the press pounced on Ali for his apparent cruelty in the ring. Of his next seven fights, often thought to be his most dominant and best technical performances, he fought four of them in other countries. To some extent, he scheduled the fights abroad in an effort to gain global recognition as world champion. But he was also escaping the unfriendly U.S. audience, which had become hostile to his beliefs and his ring performances. And the situation was only getting worse.

A new national crisis was competing with the civil rights movement for time on television news broadcasts in the mid 1960s: war in the southeast Asian nation of Vietnam. Once a French colony known as Indochina, Vietnam was torn apart by a communist revolution. The U.S. government incorrectly believed that either the Soviet Union or China was behind the efforts of the communist forces of North Vietnam, called the Vietcong, who were invading South Vietnam. In reality, the revolution had the support of a majority of people in South Vietnam as well. But the U.S. government's fear of communism was strong enough that, by 1964, President Johnson had committed large numbers of U.S. troops to the war effort on the side of an unpopular Southern regime. By June 1965, U.S. troops were fighting an all-out air and ground war halfway around the world.

As the war continued, and the casualties multiplied, the U.S. government drafted civilians to fill in the ranks. Able-bodied men were asked to take an IQ test to determine who was fit for military service and who was exempt. In January of 1964, Ali took the test and, to his embarrassment, failed. Again, it seems that his dyslexia is the best explanation for his failure, but the army simply gave him a 1-Y classification stating that he was "not qualified under current standards for service in the armed forces." By 1966, however, President Johnson needed even more soldiers and lowered the IQ standards to allow more men to be drafted. Under the new standards, Ali was given a 1-A classification. He was eligible to fight. But now, with the Nation of Islam's support, he spoke out against the war and hinted that he would refuse to serve if drafted. In doing so, he issued one of the most famous statements of the Vietnam era: "Man, I ain't got no quarrel with them Vietcong."[13]

Concerned that helping the United States gain victory on foreign battlefields would distract lawmakers from fighting racial discrimination at home, prominent members of the Nation of Islam had a long history of speaking out against U.S. military action. Elijah Muhammad had served a prison sentence during World War II for refusing to fight and, during the Korean War, Malcolm X claimed that his Muslim beliefs made him a "conscientious objector," legally exempt from military service under the U.S. Constitution. But in 1966, few other civil rights organizations shared the Nation's views on the war. SNCC spokesman Stokely Carmichael did issue a statement criticizing the escalation of the war—"Ain't no Vietcong ever called me nigger. . . . I will not fight in Vietnam and run in Georgia"—but he was scorned by most black leaders who believed his criticisms hurt their cause. A year later, Martin Luther King, Jr., would call the U.S. government "the greatest purveyor of violence in the world today,"[14] but even he was quiet about the war in 1966. Meanwhile, federal policies like the 2-S deferment, which exempted college students (mostly wealthy and mostly white) from mandatory service in the armed forces, resulted in a disproportionate number of poor African-Americans fighting in Vietnam. An equally disproportionate number were dying on the battlefields.

No longer simply a misguided black athlete with dangerous religious beliefs, Ali was now considered an enemy of the U.S. government and a traitor to the soldiers giving their lives for their country in the jungles of Vietnam. The public remembered Joe Louis's efforts during World War II and felt that Ali was not living up to the standards Louis set. Like track star Jesse Owens, who countered Adolf Hitler's racism by winning four gold medals at the 1936 Olympics in Nazi Germany, Louis scored moral victories for the United States when he defeated the German boxer Max Schmeling and the Italian giant Primo Carnera in the years leading up to World War II. During the war, the "Brown Bomber" continued his patriotic mission as a member of the Special Forces. His job was simply to entertain the troops with boxing exhibitions, but Louis went beyond the call of duty when he donated his fight purses to the war effort. "There has never been a champion like Joe Louis in the ring,"[15] newspaper reporters chimed. And the United States agreed.

But Ali ignored Joe Louis's example and the criticisms of his countrymen to follow his conscience. For his political views, he was compared to the "hippie" counter-culture blossoming in the late 1960s and was even called "the Fifth Beatle."[16] Like the British rock band, he was now regarded as a symbol of the confused, revolutionary times in which he lived, and the enemy of an older, more conservative generation.

On March 17, 1966, Ali appeared before a Louisville draft board claiming ineligibility for military service. In an attempt to avoid controversy, he justified his exemption request by announcing that he had to continue boxing to support his parents. The board rejected his claims. In August, he appeared before the Kentucky State Circuit Court and cited his religious convictions as grounds for conscientious objector status. He quoted Qur'an passages to Judge Lawrence Gauman, highlighting the Muslim prohibition against fighting in any war "on the side of nonbelievers." "This is there before I was born," Ali said when he was finished reading, "and it will be there when I'm dead and we believe in not only part of it, but all of it."[17] Gauman, to everyone's surprise, ruled in Ali's favor. But the U.S. Department of Justice sent a letter to the draft board countering Gauman's decision, and the draft board rejected Ali's request.

*Ali surrounded by a crowd after refusing to join
the army at the induction center in Houston, Texas*

As the draft controversies raged, Ali's contract with
the Louisville Sponsoring Group finally expired, and he
chose Herbert Muhammad as his new manager, keeping
Dundee close as his trainer and head cornerman. The
results were more of the same: In March 1966, he faced
George Chuvalo in Toronto—after boxing officials refused to let him fight Ernie Terrell in the United States—
and won a fifteen-round decision. After the fight, he met
with Howard Cosell for yet another entertaining interview in the now famous Cosell-Ali series. The Champ
held up his protective metal cup during the broadcast,
which was visibly dented, to prove that Chuvalo had
been hitting him with low blows. Following the Chuvalo

fight, he stomped through Henry Cooper for a second time, then Brian London—both matches in England—and finished off the road trip with a victory over Karl Mildenberger in Frankfurt, Germany. Returning to Houston, he beat heavy-puncher Cleveland "Big Cat" Williams in a fast, three-round technical knockout that many boxing experts credit as his finest technical performance.

As 1966 drew to a close, Ali was invincible in the ring, but his problems with the U.S. government were just beginning. Reacting to the civil rights and antiwar movements dividing the nation, President Johnson and J. Edgar Hoover, head of the Federal Bureau of Investigations, began surveillance on a number of disruptive public figures including Martin Luther King, Jr., and Muhammad Ali. Hoover zeroed in on Ali's seven traffic violations—he had always been a reckless driver with his tour bus—his connections to boxing promoters, and his connections to the Nation of Islam, searching for a weakness he could use to discredit the boxer and his political views.

With the FBI breathing down his neck, Ali finally faced Ernie Terrell for the World Boxing Association belt. The championship had been bestowed on Terrell in 1964 when Sonny Liston bypassed Terrell, the top contender, to fight Ali first. Now Terrell made the same mistake that Floyd Patterson had made a year earlier: He characterized his fight with Ali as a battle between good and evil, between a patriot and a coward. He refused to call Ali by his new name, stubbornly calling him "Clay" in press conferences. Ali beat the fighter senseless but refused to let him fall. He held Terrell up to humiliate him and continue his punishment. "What's my name?" he asked as he punched.[18] Terrell was in the wrong place at the wrong time. For fifteen rounds he was the target of Ali's fury. The press finally had evidence to support its theory that the racist, draft-dodging Muhammad Ali was also a mean-spirited bully.

And then came the climax. The Louisville Draft Board announced April 11 as the date of Ali's physical examination and induction into the military. At his lawyer's request, Ali changed his official residence to the city of Houston, Texas, hoping for a more lenient ruling from the Houston Draft Board. His physical was rescheduled for April 28. On that morning in Houston, he joined twenty-five other draftees headed for basic training. He passed his physical and then, when the name "Cassius Marcellus Clay" was called, he refused to take the symbolic step forward to complete the induction ceremony. Even though military officials promised him a spot in the Special Forces as an entertainer just as Joe Louis had been, he would not answer the call to arms. Ten days later, he was indicted by a federal grand jury for draft evasion.

In early June, Ali met with a number of prominent African-American athletes including football star Jim Brown and basketball greats Bill Russell and Lew Alcindor (who later converted to Islam and took the name Kareem Abdul-Jabbar) to discuss the impact of his actions on the civil rights movement. The athletes supported Ali's decision, and Russell came out of the meeting with deep respect for the strength of Ali's religious convictions: "He has something very few people I know possess. He has an absolute and sincere faith."[19]

Unfortunately, not everyone was as convinced of Ali's sincerity. On June 20, he was convicted of draft evasion by a jury that doubted the Nation of Islam's religious foundations. One hour later, the New York State Athletic Commission voided his boxing license and took back his championship belt. Every other state athletic commission followed New York's lead. Since the court also took away his passport as part of the punishment, the world champion was now effectively barred from every boxing ring in the world. Worse than that, Ali faced a $10,000 fine and a possible five-year prison term. Hoping to receive a more lenient sentence, Ali pleaded with his anti-war supporters not to protest outside the courthouse. In addition, the court found that Ali's phone had been illegally tapped by the FBI during its investigations, making special note of a recorded conversation between Ali and Martin Luther King, Jr. But he received a very severe penalty despite these two developments. The government, led by the prominent African-American prosecutor Thurgood Marshall, was making an example of Ali to discourage other conscientious objectors. Ali's attorneys immediately appealed the decision to a higher court, postponing his prison term indefinitely.

Meanwhile, a national tournament was held to find a new champion after Ali was stripped of his belt. But any claim to the title would be immediately disputed by a number of civil rights organizations, including SNCC and CORE, who announced that "white America cannot tell black people who deserves to be the world champion and decide for black people who the world's champion is."[20] Ali had become a national symbol, despised by the older white people who were running the country, but suddenly revered by African-Americans and young whites for his courage in taking on the U.S. government. "To the late-1960s white counterculture," writes historian Michael Oriard, "Ali surely was identified more with the anti-war movement than with black separatism; to blacks during this same period he surely represented chiefly racial pride."[21] So in a time of great social upheaval throughout the United States, Ali was suddenly the hero of every reformer and radical. No longer just a charismatic boxer, he had suddenly become a major force of change in U.S. culture.

5

The Return

It was not easy for Ali to give up the sport he loved while he waited for higher courts to hear his appeal. Without boxing as a source of income, he did not know how he would survive. But true to form, he added his own special complications to the situation. On August 17, 1967, two months after he was convicted of draft evasion, Ali married Belinda Boyd, a seventeen-year-old employee at a Muslim bakery in Chicago. Belinda was, in many ways, a perfect match for Ali. She was a devoted follower of Elijah Muhammad. She was a talented student at the University of Islam, Elijah's school. She was strong-willed and brave, and she wore the traditional *hijab* as a symbol of her orthodox Islamic beliefs. And she was a tall, striking beauty. Unfortunately, with the prohibitions on Ali's fighting career, the young couple would have to struggle through difficult times early in their relationship.

Ali with his wife Belinda, whom he married in 1967. She was but seventeen at the time.

"Standing up for my religion made me happy," Ali has said in recent years. "It wasn't a sacrifice. When people got drafted and sent to Vietnam and didn't understand what the killing was about and came home with one leg and couldn't get jobs, that was a sacrifice. But I believed in what I was doing, so no matter what the government did to me, it wasn't a loss."[1] In many ways, Ali's exile from the boxing ring represented his greatest achievement. When the public saw that Ali was willing to give up his livelihood and his glory for his religious beliefs, when people realized that he was actually losing more by accepting his punishment than he would have lost if he had followed Joe Louis's example and entered

66

the Special Services, they gained a new respect for him. Civil rights activist groups such as CORE supported his decisions from the very beginning. But as the exile continued, antiwar politicians, writers, and even Christian leaders came to Ali's defense.

The public's increasing acceptance of Ali's stand against the Vietnam War signaled a new trend of antiwar protests throughout the country. In 1967, more than 75,000 people assembled at the Lincoln Memorial in Washington, D.C., demanding that the government pull U.S. troops out of Southeast Asia. The Johnson administration ignored the protest, claiming that the war was nearly over. But at the end of January 1968, during the Vietnamese holiday known as Tet, North Vietnamese forces accomplished a well-organized attack on several U.S. military installations. The strength of the attack, called the Tet Offensive, proved that the North Vietnamese were still strong, and that the Johnson administration had been hiding the truth about the war. After watching footage of the Tet Offensive, CBS news anchor Walter Cronkite announced, "For every means we have to escalate [the war], the enemy can match us. . . . To say that we are mired in stalemate seems the only realistic, yet unsatisfactory, conclusion."[2] Suddenly, for the first time in its history, the United States seemed to be involved in a war it could not win.

But Johnson would not give up. In March, he called in the Armed Reserves to support the thousands of U.S. troops already fighting in the Vietnamese jungles. By the end of the month, after a year of deadly catastrophe in Vietnam, public opinion turned against Lyndon Johnson. On March 31, he made the most famous announcement of his presidency: "I shall not seek and I will not accept the nomination of my party for another term."[3] With Johnson out of the presidential race, the hope of many voters—particularly young, antiwar voters—rested with Senator Robert F. Kennedy. However, Robert was to suffer the same fate as his brother, President John F. Kennedy. He was shot three times by an assassin during a campaign celebration on June 5; he died the next day. The violence continued later in the month, at the Democratic National Convention in Chicago. Inside the convention hall, delegates argued bitterly over U.S. involvement in Vietnam. On the streets outside, Chicago police officers attacked antiwar protesters. And the violence continued after the convention, and after the election. Far from bringing the war to a peaceful conclusion, newly elected President Richard M. Nixon escalated the war again by authorizing massive bombing raids in North Vietnam as well as in the nations of Cambodia and Laos. Finally, in 1970, soldiers of the National Guard shot and killed four protesting students at Kent State University in Ohio and Jackson State College in Mississippi.

And the civil rights movement did not fare much better. Having already lost activist Medgar Evers to an assassin's bullet in 1963, and Malcolm X in 1965, the movement was hardest hit on April 4, 1968, when Martin Luther King, Jr., was shot and killed in Memphis, Tennessee. At this point, some black activists such as SNCC leader Robert Moses simply gave up on the United States and moved to Africa. With the Civil Rights Act of 1964 and the Voting Rights Act of 1965—which eliminated discriminatory practices in the enrollment of voters—the government removed the largest remaining legal barriers to integration. But African-American leaders still felt that true equality was out of reach. In the late 1960s, race riots leveled black communities in major U.S. cities: New York in 1964, Los Angeles in 1965, Detroit in 1967, and hundreds of smaller outbursts following King's assassination.

Following Ali's lead, black athletes took a more active role in the increasingly radical civil rights upheaval of the late 1960s. In 1968, basketball star Lew Alcindor led a boycott of black athletes against the Summer Olympics in Mexico City to protest the stubborn remnants of discrimination in U.S. society. And two black athletes who decided to attend the Games, track stars Tommie Smith and John Carlos, shocked and embarrassed the United States when they performed the Black Power salute— heads down, clenched fists in black gloves held above their heads—as they accepted their gold and silver medals.

As the first athlete to support black nationalism, and the first high-profile celebrity to speak out against the Vietnam War, Ali inspired thousands, like Alcindor, to act on their beliefs. Now that others were taking part in civil rights and antiwar protests, he slowly backed away from the controversy. Early in his exile, he performed lectures on a circuit of the nation's colleges. Speaking about his religious beliefs and his stand against the Vietnam War, Ali's quick mind and wonderful sense of humor served him well. He attracted large crowds for his appearances and captivated his listeners with his candid remarks on the nation's problems. But he was not making enough money to support himself and Belinda, so he turned his attention to other projects: a short film of his life entitled *A/K/A Cassius Clay*, a brief engagement as the star of the Broadway musical *Buck White* (for which even his singing received decent reviews), and an early computer-simulation of a fight between himself and the retired champion Rocky Marciano for British and U.S. television.

Still harassed for his views—in December 1968, he spent ten days in a Dade County, Florida, jail for driving without a valid license, a relatively minor offense—and troubled by his crumbling financial situation, Ali was finally becoming discouraged and restless. In early 1969, he admitted to Howard Cosell that he wanted to return to the boxing ring. He needed money, as he admitted, but he also needed to be a part of the action again. Elijah supported Ali's legal battle, which would soon reach the U.S. Supreme Court. But for his statements to Cosell, Ali was banished from the Nation of Islam for one year.

Elijah Muhammad had always been an outspoken critic of professional athletics, believing that sports diverted attention from Allah and the Nation. He had allowed Ali to continue his boxing career before the exile because Ali attracted publicity for the Nation. But once boxing officials forced Ali to abandon his sport, Elijah saw no reason for Ali to box again. He considered Ali's eagerness to box a betrayal of the Nation's principles. In the April 4, 1969, issue of the Nation's newspaper, *Muhammad Speaks*, Elijah expressed his anger in the article "We Tell the World We're Not with Muhammad Ali":

> *Mr. Muhammad Ali shall not be recognized with us under the holy name Muhammad Ali. We call him Cassius Clay. We take away the name of Allah from him until he proves himself worthy of that name. . . . We, the Muslims, are not with Muhammad Ali in the desire to work in the sports world "for the sake of a leetle money."*[4]

Elijah's son, Herbert Muhammad, was also banished for supporting Ali's decision to appear in the musical *Buck White*. Ali's brother Rahaman avoided the controversy and remained loyal to Elijah's teachings.

Even though Rahaman remained, at least publicly, "against" his brother, Ali's private life was more settled during his banishment than it had been in years. Bundini was back at Ali's side now that the Fruit of Islam, his Nation-appointed guards, were no longer watching as carefully. Cash Clay appeared more frequently in his son's company. And, best of all, Ali and Belinda bought a house together in Philadelphia, a house big enough to accommodate their growing family. As the long, violent decade of the 1960s concluded, they already had three daughters—Maryum, Rasheeda, and Jamillah—and his son Muhammad Jr. was soon to follow.

Ali had reason to believe that the next decade would be better and more peaceful than the last. By early 1970, public approval for Ali's position on the Vietnam War was on the rise. And although a new heavyweight champion had been crowned (on February 16, Joe Frazier defeated Jimmy Ellis in the final round of the championship tournament), Ali still claimed the title was his. One politician, Mayor Sam Massell of Atlanta, actually found a way to turn the shift in public opinion to his own advantage and help Ali in the process. In an attempt to garner the support of Atlanta's African-American voters, Massell sponsored a bout between Ali and Jerry Quarry. Since Georgia had no boxing commissioner, there was no one to obstruct Ali's return to the ring. So Ali and Quarry signed the contract and went back to their gyms to train for a match set for October 26, 1970. Even though he was staying at the forest cabin of Georgia Senator Leroy Johnson during his preparation, Ali was not comfortable. Old resentments and racism appeared in surprising ways in the weeks before the fight. Ali received the head and body of a decapitated dog in the mail. Hiding terrorists fired gun shots near the house and then left threatening messages: "Nigger, if you don't leave Atlanta tomorrow, you gonna die. You Vietcong bastard! You draft-dodging bastard! We won't miss you

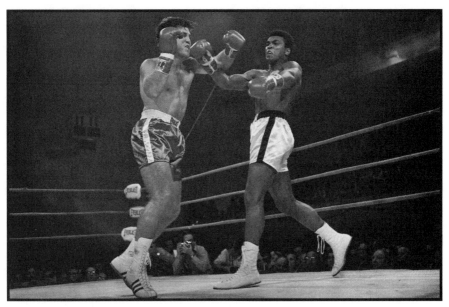

Ali and Jerry Quarry in the 1970 bout in Atlanta

next time!"[5] By the end of the training period, the senator's cabin was pitted with bullet holes.

But Ali persevered and, on October 26, tied on the gloves for the first time in more than three years. Before a packed audience and a host of African-American celebrities—including comedian Bill Cosby, actor Sidney Poitier, Reverend Jesse Jackson, and Martin Luther King, Jr.'s widow, Coretta Scott King—Ali squared off against the tough, tenacious Quarry. With Bundini chanting in the background, "Jack Johnson's ghost is watching you,"[6] Ali won the first round and fought toe to toe with Quarry in the second. But by the third round, a huge cut opened above Quarry's eye and the referee stopped the fight, awarding Ali a technical knockout. It was obvious during the fight that, after a three-year layoff, Ali did not have his old, blinding footspeed. But the hard part was over. He won a decisive victory and was off to a good start in pursuit of Joe Frazier's championship belt.

The most significant moment of the evening came after the fight, however. During the press conference, Ali was joined by Coretta Scott King and Reverend Ralph Abernathy, who presented the fighter with the "Dr. Martin Luther King Memorial Award" for his contributions to the struggle for equality. Three years earlier, Ali refused to take the symbolic first step into the Vietnam War and was nearly abandoned by his country. Now the country was slowly coming to see things his way. As public sentiment toward Vietnam shifted, Ali was poised to reclaim his status as a national hero.

Following the Quarry fight, and the post-fight festivities, members of the National Association for the Advancement of Colored People (NAACP) and Columbia University Law School pooled their resources to argue for the reinstatement of Ali's New York boxing license. The group accused the New York State Athletic Commission of subjecting Ali to harsher penalties than other boxers who committed crimes, thereby violating his constitutional right to equal protection under the Fourteenth Amendment. The federal government agreed, and Ali's New York State boxing license was returned to him in time for a December 7, 1970, fight against Oscar Bonavena at Madison Square Garden.

The Argentine fighter had already given the champion, Joe Frazier, a tough fight and was ready to do the same for Ali. He stood up to Ali's attack for fourteen rounds, but crumbled in the fifteenth, falling three times as Ali won his second technical knockout of the year. Before the exile, Ali might have beaten Bonavena more quickly, but he was still encouraged by his performance. Bonavena was a pretty good puncher, and after a long layoff, Ali learned that could he still stand up to the heaviest punches. He knew that he would need that durability, that granite chin, when he faced Joe Frazier. And he was in a big hurry to meet Frazier in the ring. More than anything in the world, Ali wanted to win his title back.

Ali's year-long banishment from the Nation of Islam was a turning point in his relationship with Elijah Muhammad. He was not vocal about his slow separation from the Nation, but by the early 1970s, it was apparent that a split was in progress. After the return of Bundini and Cash Sr. to his training sessions and fights, the next important indication was Ali's increasing openness about his charity work. Elijah preached modesty and frugality, hoping that these virtues would bring his followers a measure of financial security and independence. But Ali was not modest or frugal by nature. He bought expensive cars, he loved to travel, and he habitually gave away money to people in need. When his relationship with Elijah was at its high point, Ali was secretive about giving away money. He would organize foot-races for children in poor neighborhoods, or he would pick up hitchhikers and give them enough money to reach their destinations. But after the one-year banishment, Ali was no longer as careful. In New York after the Bonavena fight, he watched a television news story about a Jewish nursing home that was evicting elderly people who could not afford the $100,000 service fee. Following the report, he contacted the nursing home and donated an enormous sum of money on the condition that he remain anonymous. Word of his generosity leaked out anyway, and Ali was suddenly on the front page of every New York newspaper.

Another sign that Elijah and Ali were parting ways was the return of the Ali Circus, in greater numbers and variety than ever before. The entourage now included Bundini, Bingham, Dundee, Pacheco, Herbert Muhammad, Rahaman Ali, Ali's official training session time keeper Wali "Blood" Muhammad (formerly Walter Youngblood), Cuban masseur Luis Sarria, businessman Gene Kilroy, Ali's Muslim cook Lana Shabazz, and his bodyguard Howard "Pat" Patterson. Other friends and eccentrics floated in and out, depending on where Ali was and what he needed. And Howard Cosell, the sportscaster who supported Ali during his conversion to Islam and his exile from boxing and who served as Ali's straightman during his famous television tirades, was never far away.

In early 1971, with the full entourage cheering him on, Ali was ready to have fun again, to perform for his audience and entertain his fans as he had earlier in his career. So when he was challenged to a boxing match by basketball legend Wilt Chamberlain, he immediately accepted. At 7 feet 2 inches (2.18 m) and 275 pounds (124.74 kg), "Wilt the Stilt" was hardly designed for the ring, but he trained hard for the match and really thought he'd give Ali a tough fight. Until the pre-fight press conference. When the treelike basketball star walked into the crowded conference room, Ali yelled "Timber!" As the reporters laughed, Chamberlain called off the fight.[7]

Ali was not too disappointed when Chamberlain backed out, however. There were much bigger events on the horizon. On December 30, 1970, he had signed a contract worth $2.5 million to fight Joe Frazier for the title. The match, already billed as the "Fight of the Century" by promoters and the press, was scheduled for March 8, 1971, at Madison Square Garden. It promised to be a bigger show than any Ali had ever been involved with, and a tougher fight.

Joe Frazier, whose father was a poor farmer and bootlegger, was born in Beaufort, South Carolina. He had moved to Philadelphia as he began his climb to the top of the boxing ranks. He won the heavyweight gold medal at the Tokyo Olympics of 1964, even though he was relatively small in stature—5 feet 11 inches (1.8 m), 205 pounds (93 kg). When he signed the contract to fight Ali, he was, like Ali, undefeated in his professional career. But he knew that he would not be considered the real champion until he had beaten Ali in the ring.

According to Frazier, the two fighters negotiated the fight arrangements as friends:

We talked about how much we were going to make out of our fight. We were laughin' and havin' fun. We were friends, we were great friends. I said, "Why not? Come on, man, let's do it!" He was a brother. He called me Joe: "Hey, Smokin' Joe!" In New York we were gonna put on this commotion.[8]

But Ali and Frazier had different definitions of the word "commotion." Frazier was a quiet, hardworking brawler. Ali was a flashy, athletic boxer with a big mouth. When Ali started his own pre-fight promotion by attacking Frazier—"He ain't the champ, he's the chump. I'm the people's champ!"[9]—Frazier felt betrayed. When Ali said that all black people were rooting for him, and that Frazier was an ignorant "Uncle Tom," Frazier got angry. And he channeled his anger into his training.

The stars were out on the night of March 8, 1971. Madison Square Garden was buzzing with excitement as the Hollywood celebrities filed into their ringside seats. Cultural icons Woody Allen, Danny Kaye, and Andy

Williams had tickets, but Diana Ross and Dustin Hoffman did not and were sent home for trying to crash the press box. Singer Frank Sinatra was hired by *Life* magazine to photograph the match. Actor Burt Lancaster was a celebrity TV commentator. Everyone was dressed in his or her finest, most colorful clothes. And 300 million people were watching the event on closed-circuit televisions in forty-six different countries. There had never been, and perhaps there has never been since, a sporting event of this magnitude.

Ali entered the arena wearing a red robe and red trunks with red tassels hanging from his trademark white shoes. From the moment he stepped into the ring, he danced in wide circles, playing to the crowd. Frazier, wearing a green and yellow robe and the same color trunks, was quiet and intense. Ali got off to a fast start in the fight, jabbing Frazier's face, pulling at Frazier's head, and winning the first five rounds. Frazier won the next five with persistent attacks, his head kept low, like a charging bull. Normally a quiet, businesslike fighter, Frazier was talking as much as Ali. When Ali said, midway through the fight, "You're crazy coming after me," Frazier responded, "That's right, man. I'm crazy."[10] By the eleventh round, a pattern was forming: Ali was attacking Frazier's face while Frazier pounded Ali's hips. In what is now known as "the Gruesome Eleventh," or "The Long Walk," Ali's hips nearly gave out. His legs began to wobble. But, as he lost his quickness with age, Ali trained himself to take more punches. So he was able to survive Frazier's onslaught and actually came back to win the twelfth round. In the thirteenth—as Bundini chanted, "God's in your corner!"[11]—Ali took another pounding, but Frazier suffered too. His face was swollen now, deformed. Neither man had much strength left. They fought fourteen rounds to a draw. They would both

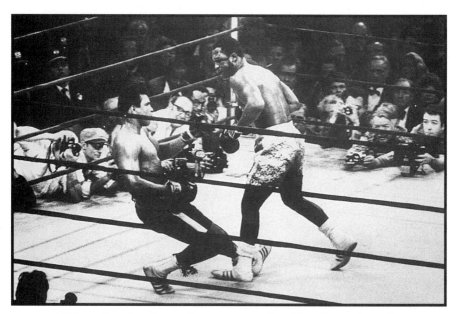

Ali leaning back on the ropes as Joe Frazier takes the opportunity to beat him and become the heavyweight champion in 1971

spend the night in the hospital, recovering from the contest. But the winner of the fifteenth round would take home the belt. Ali's legs were wobbling again, and Frazier connected with one punch, a left hook, that sent Ali to the canvas. He recovered quickly and was standing as the referee counted, but it was too late. The knockdown sealed the decision for Frazier. Ali lost the first fight of his professional career, and Joe Frazier was still the heavyweight champion of the world.

During the fight, Frazier marveled at Ali's ability to take a punch. But after the fight and for many years to come, all he could talk about was how poorly Ali had treated him during the fight buildup, and how proud he was to have humbled the former champion: "I used to watch him on television, talking about me before the fight, and I'd say, 'God, give him to me; I want him so bad.' But I shut his mouth. Yes, I did."[12] Ali was quieter after the fight, however. He was more philosophical about his first professional loss as he put his boxing career in perspective for the reporters: "Presidents get assassinated, civil rights leaders get assassinated. The world goes on. You'll all be writing about something else soon. I had my day. You lose, you don't shoot yourself."[13]

Certainly, as Ali suggested, his first loss was not as important as the horrible tragedies of the previous decade. But Ali could not hide his disappointment or his renewed hunger for the belt. Before the press conference was over, Ali promised the world that there would be an Ali-Frazier rematch.

6

Victories

Losing to Joe Frazier was hard on Ali, but he was dealing with harder issues in the spring of 1971. Even though he was back in the ring, and back in the spotlight, the draft evasion controversy was not over. His case, after numerous appeals, was now before the Supreme Court. If the court ruled in his favor, the charges would be dropped. If the court ruled against him, he could serve a five-year jail term. On April 19, 1971, U.S. Solicitor General Ernest Griswold and Ali's attorney Chauncey Eskridge read their opening statements to an eight-member court (the ninth justice, Thurgood Marshall, did not sit on the case since he was chief prosecutor during the original trial in Houston). Griswold convinced the court that since Ali, according to Islamic teachings, would fight in any war waged by Allah, he was not a true conscientious objector. This argument, coupled with the fear that more African-Americans would join the Nation of Islam simply to avoid military service, persuaded the court to rule against Ali. But when Justice John Harlan sat to write the court's opinion, his clerks, who sided with Ali, suggested that he first read Malcolm X's autobiography, and Elijah Muhammad's *Message to the Black Man in America* before making his final decision. The clerks' tactics succeeded. The books changed Harlan's opinion of the Nation of Islam and of Ali. When he explained his new objections to the verdict, he split the court evenly with four judges supporting Ali's defense and four supporting the prosecution. To break the tie, Justice Potter Stewart found a flaw in the court's documentation, a useful loophole for the Ali supporters. So on June 28, 1971, in the case of *Clay v. United States*, the Supreme Court voted unanimously to drop the charges against Ali. The justices did not declare Ali a true conscientious objector; they merely decided that the government failed to properly file its complaints against Ali. The decision did not set many precedents for later cases, but it did clarify the basic criteria for deciding the value of a person's claims to conscientious objector status. Since the *Clay* case, a conscientious objector must prove that his or her beliefs are based in religion, that he or she is sincere in those beliefs, and that he or she opposes war in any form.

Ignoring the technicalities of the decision, Ali claimed a complete victory: "I thank Allah and I thank the Supreme Court for recognizing the sincerity of the religious teachings I've accepted."[1] But just as Ali was breathing his sigh of relief, other Vietnam War protesters were losing ground. On June 28, 1971, the same day that the *Clay* verdict was read, Daniel Ellsberg was indicted for passing top-secret government documents, known as the "Pentagon Papers," to major national newspapers. The "Pentagon Papers" revealed that the government had been hiding important information about the Vietnam War from the public. The next day, the Supreme Court accepted an emergency petition from the Justice Department to remove protesting war veterans from the Mall in Washington, D.C. The Vietnam controversies continued to rage throughout the early 1970s.

But Ali moved on after the Supreme Court ruling, and reenergized his pursuit of Frazier's title. On July 26, at the Houston Astrodome, he faced his boyhood friend and former Louisville sparring partner Jimmy Ellis, the man Frazier had beaten to earn his heavyweight title. Ali defeated Ellis in twelve rounds. Then came Buster Mathis in November. Frazier had beaten Mathis for the first half of his world title while Ali was banned from the ring. Now Mathis needed money and saw his fight with Ali as a financial windfall. Ali genuinely liked Mathis, knew Mathis was out of shape, and went easy on him for a twelve-round decision. Suddenly, the same writers who criticized Ali for his viciousness against Floyd Patterson and Ernie Terrell criticized him for laying off Mathis. But Ali the showman proved there was a limit to his showmanship—he would not hurt a man who was already down. "I don't care about looking good for the fans," he said. "I got to look good to God. I got to sleep at night."[2]

Even without the championship belt, Ali was finding it easier to sleep during this period of his life. His popularity in the United States was rising again; the spotlight was friendly once more. In August of 1972, after winning a few more fights against old opponents like George Chuvalo and Jerry Quarry, the Warner Brothers movie company approached Ali with a $250,000 contract to star in an upcoming movie. *Heaven Can Wait* was originally to be the story of a boxer who dies, is brought back to life, and wins the heavyweight championship. Ali loved the idea, and was beginning to crave Hollywood stardom.

But Elijah Muhammad still had some influence over Ali's decisions, and he put a stop to the project. The Nation of Islam, Elijah said, did not believe in the movie's afterlife premise. So Ali abandoned the project (which later became the story of a football quarterback played by Warren Beatty) and turned his attention to the construction of his training camp in the woods in Deer Lake, Pennsylvania, a sprawling compound of buildings devoted to Ali and his entourage, and always open to the public.

After a series of easy fights, Ali signed on for a March 31 bout in San Diego, a fight that was supposed to be another opportunity for him to hone his skills. (Frazier, meanwhile, was in no hurry to grant Ali a rematch.) His opponent was a physically imposing ex-Marine named Ken Norton, who had sparred with Frazier and fought a few minor professional bouts. He had an awkward boxing style but was a strong puncher. He also had a brilliant trainer in Eddie Futch. While Ali was lazy about his training, Norton worked hard and listened closely as Futch described Ali's weakness: Ali exposed the right side of his face because he did not keep his hands up. To make matters worse, Ali sprained his ankle while golfing in San Diego shortly before the fight.

When the bell sounded for round one, Norton pursued a less mobile Ali and pounded his jaw, just as Futch had advised. After round two, Ali returned to his corner complaining that he could move his jawbone with his tongue, that his jaw was in fact broken. But Ali refused to stop the fight. He survived the full twelve rounds, avoiding shots aimed at his face and fought through the agony of his injury. Norton won the judges' decision, but the courage Ali displayed in finishing the bout won him even more admirers. According to fight doctor Ferdie Pacheco, "In losing to Norton, he actually won—he won the respect of his boxing peers. They knew from the Frazier fight that he was tough, from the Norton fight they learned *how* tough."[3]

Ali was rushed into surgery after the fight so that doctors could reset his jawbone. After the procedure, with his mouth wired shut to allow the bone to heal, he mumbled out a statement of his own:

I want to thank Kenny Norton. Learned a very important lesson from him. From now on, I'll be a good old man. Like Archie Moore. I'll eat the right foods, run ten miles a day. Do thousands of situps, hundreds of rounds of sparrin' and bag work. And you white folks'll find out what this old spade has left.[4]

Ali did indeed train hard after the fight, and so did Norton. Their rematch on September 30, 1973, was a contest between two conditioned, well-prepared athletes. As in the first match, Ali had problems countering Norton's awkward style. Going into the twelfth round, the fight was even. But Ali won the twelfth round and the fight by a narrow margin and a unanimous decision. A month later, he defeated Rudi Lubbers in Jakarta, Indonesia. Finally, Smokin' Joe Frazier agreed to a rematch.

But Frazier was no longer champion. On January 22, 1973, in Kingston, Jamaica, he had fallen six times in two rounds against a mean, young punching machine named George Foreman. As a result, the stakes were much lower for this second fight. Yet the fighters went out of their way to maintain the suspense of their rivalry. During a January 23, 1974, joint interview with Howard Cosell on ABC, Frazier mentioned Ali's brief stay in the hospital after their first matchup. Ali called Frazier "ignorant" and reminded Frazier that he spent three weeks in the hospital after the fight.[5] In the confusion that followed, Frazier faced off with Rahaman Ali, who was standing in the wings of the studio. When Muhammad Ali tried to ease the tension, restraining Frazier in a playful wrestling hold, Frazier tossed Ali to the floor. Both Ali and Frazier were fined $5,000 by the New York State Athletic Commission for their behavior. Belt or no belt, these two champions were not going to take their next meeting lightly.

Unfortunately for Frazier, he fought a different Ali in the second match. In 1971, Ali had not been ready to face a champion of Frazier's caliber. He was still recovering from his three-year layoff and learning to box on slower feet. Even then he survived Frazier's attacks and lost in the final round. But in Madison Square Garden on January 28, 1974, more than a year after Frazier lost the title to Foreman, Ali was ready for his opponent. He weighed in at 212 pounds (96.16 kg), two pounds (.9 kg) over his weight for the first Liston fight. And he had a strategy: He would jab Frazier into submission, avoid Frazier's rushes, protect his hips, and pull Frazier's head down when he got too close—an illegal but effective maneuver. Frazier never had much of a chance. In the second round, it even looked as if Ali would knock Smokin' Joe down. But referee Tony Perez mistakenly separated the fighters, believing that he heard the end-of-round bell. Ali complained about Perez's costly error, of course, but scored a decisive victory on points anyway.

His victory over Frazier marked the end of a long, difficult era for Muhammad Ali. When he was stripped of his title in 1967, he became the "what-if" champion, like a ghost haunting the sport of boxing. Ali joined his supporters and his detractors in asking: What if he were allowed to fight? Would he still be champion? In particular, Ali's absence haunted Joe Frazier, whose own claim to the title was questioned by everyone from boxing fans to civil rights groups. Even after their first meeting, boxing fans were still left wondering if Frazier could have beaten Ali in his prime, in 1967, when he was so fast that no one could touch him. The second fight laid those questions to rest. Muhammad Ali was still a great fighter, though a slower fighter, and was still a serious contender for the title. Yes, he could still be champion.

The early months of 1974 also marked the end of an era for the nation. In February, the House of Representatives began an investigation into the campaign practices of President Richard Nixon. Before this investigation, Nixon was criticized for pushing the Vietnam War beyond Vietnamese borders and into neighboring Cambodia and Laos. After years of angry debate, he finally signed a cease-fire agreement in 1973 and pulled all remaining U.S. troops out of Vietnam, ending U.S. participation in the conflict. The Watergate scandal followed on the heels of the war controversy. By July 1974, the Judiciary Committee found that Nixon had authorized illegal spying activities at the Watergate Hotel in Washington, D.C., the headquarters of the Democratic Party. The committee also found Nixon guilty of obstructing federal investigations, abusing his power as president, and defying congressional orders. Realizing that he would be forced out of office for his role in the scandals, Nixon resigned on August 8, 1974, leaving Vice President Gerald Ford to assume the presidency. With the resignation of the last president to support U.S. military involvement in Southeast Asia, the Vietnam era drew to a close.

Now that Ali had defeated Joe Frazier and outlasted the politicians who supported the war he refused to fight, he was ready to reclaim his title as the "people's champ," the most popular heavyweight champion of all time. The only person standing in his way was a 6-foot 3-inch (1.9-m), 220-pound (99.8-kg) fighter named George Foreman.

George Foreman and Ali were similar in size and build when they matched up in 1974.

Foreman's past was shady and contributed to his reputation as the meanest boxer since Sonny Liston, with whom he trained for a short time. After a difficult childhood, when he was repeatedly in trouble with the law for an assortment of crimes, Foreman learned to box. His hero, of course, was a handsome, brash young fighter named Cassius Clay. Boxing gave Foreman discipline and an outlet for his energies. In 1968, he was asked to represent the United States at the Olympics in Mexico City and won the heavyweight gold medal. He began his professional career in devastating fashion, knocking out eleven men and winning two decisions in 1969. And he continued to wreak havoc through the early 1970s, beating Frazier easily in a 1973 championship fight. By 1974, Foreman's record stood at forty wins, no losses, thirty-seven knockouts, and the heavyweight title. Not one of his last eight fights extended past the third round.

Given the reputations of the two boxers, a simple Ali-Foreman bout would have been an enormous boxing event. But newcomer Don King was the fight's promoter, and King was ready to put on a bigger show than even Ali could have imagined. An ex-bookie who had spent time in jail for manslaughter, King decided to make a new name for himself in the boxing world, arranging fights and attracting crowds. Ali-Foreman was his first large production, and he was after something that had never been tried before: a boxing match designed to inspire unity between Africans and African-Americans.

While selecting a venue for the fight, King met with representatives of Mobutu Sese Seko, the corrupt, dictatorial president of the African nation of Zaire. Mobutu wanted to host the fight as a way to generate publicity for his country. The setting was just right for the all-black event King planned, a fight that would include two black fighters, a black referee, and King himself as the first major black promoter in boxing. To complete the lineup for the event, which Ali named "The Rumble in the Jungle," King organized a concert for black musicians including singer James Brown and blues legend B.B. King. And he promised Ali and Foreman $5 million each when they signed on.

Mobutu, who wanted to convince the world that Zaire was a healthy, thriving nation under his guidance, rounded up every criminal, political opponent, and unsavory character in the capital city of Kinshasa and imprisoned them until the fight was over and the foreign press was gone. Ali and the rest of the foreign visitors who flooded the nation saw the best that Mobutu's Zaire could offer, and Ali was almost as amazed by the citizens of Zaire as they were by him.

"I used to think Africans were savages," he said. "But now that I'm here, I've learned that Africans are wiser than we are. They speak English and two or three more languages. Ain't that something? We in America are the savages."[6]

Mobutu invited both fighters to stay at his private compound in N'Sele, forty miles from Kinshasa. Ali accepted the invitation but Foreman grew restless in quiet N'Sele and returned to the Intercontinental Hotel in Kinshasa. Foreman was reserved, even abrupt with reporters. To the people of Zaire, he appeared unfriendly. In contrast, Ali played to the crowd. Stories of his brave conversion to Islam and his victory over the U.S. government had traveled to Zaire, and he was considered a living hero. And Ali certainly encouraged this view. He traveled to poor villages when he was not training. He played with children and entertained throngs of followers as he jogged through the streets near his camp. Everywhere he went, he led the popular cheer, "Ali, bomaye!"—ALI-BOOM-AY-YEE—"Ali, kill him!"

Ali training in Zaire before the "Rumble in the Jungle"

The fighters' training sessions were intense, heavily publicized events and handlers in both camps competed for press time and plotted to unnerve the opponent. From the Ali entourage, Bundini was the most active. According to Ferdie Pacheco, he worked his way into the Intercontinental Hotel and started rumors about poison in Foreman's food.[7] To Ali's delight, Foreman showed signs of impatience with the buildup to the fight, with the media attention, and with Bundini's schemes. Then, eight days before the fight, just as Foreman was reaching peak condition, he was cut above the eye during a sparring session. The match had to be postponed a full month and was rescheduled for October 30. Neither fighter was happy about the delay. Zaire was a poor nation and a difficult place to live, even for the guests of honor. But Foreman seemed the most upset, sulking as Ali continued to train and antagonize his opponent: "George Foreman is nothing but a big mummy. I've officially named him 'The Mummy.' He moves like a slow mummy and there ain't no mummy gonna whup the great Muhammad Ali."[8] And then came the poetry: "You think the world was shocked when Nixon resigned? Wait till I whup George Foreman's behind."[9]

The bout was scheduled to start at four o'clock in the morning on October 30 to allow closed-circuit television audiences in the United States to see the fight live. Even at that early hour, with dark thunderclouds hovering overhead, the football stadium in Kinshasa was packed with 60,000 fans chanting "Ali, bomaye!" while Foreman's entourage circled the stadium shouting their own prediction: "Oh yez, oh yez, Ali in three!"[10]

Dundee advised Ali to box as he had against Sonny Liston: to rely on his quick jabs and much quicker feet to exhaust Foreman with his constant motion. Foreman, coached by Dick Sadler and Archie Moore, was ready to come out punching. Ali announced before the fight that he would throw a sharp right hand as the bell sounded, just to remind Foreman that he was now fighting a real champion. And that is exactly what Ali did: He hit Foreman with a hard right to open the bout and then followed Dundee's stick-and-move strategy, surprising the experts by winning the first round. But Ali knew he no longer had the speed and stamina to fight in his old style for twelve rounds against Big George Foreman.

To compensate for his aging legs, Ali performed yet another magic trick in a career that seemed, more than ever, the stuff of legend: He invented a new style of boxing in the second round of the Rumble in the Jungle. He leaned back against the ropes and allowed Foreman, boxing's heaviest hitter, to pound at him for the next six rounds. "Man, that ain't nothing, George. They told me you could punch," he said as he protected his head from Foreman's fists.[11] Dundee and Bundini begged Ali to get off the ropes and fight, but Ali ignored them. "I know what I'm doing," he said.[12] Every so often, he threw a careful, perfect jab at Foreman's face. Otherwise he had turned himself into a human punching bag. Ali would later call his strategy "rope-a-dope," but for seven rounds it seemed like suicide to everyone watching. By the eighth round, however, Foreman's punches had less force behind them. He had hit Ali so many times that he was fatigued. Suddenly the crowd realized the strategy behind rope-a-dope. Ali had forced Foreman to attack for seven full rounds, while he leaned back on the ropes, blocked punches, and conserved energy. As soon as Foreman's strength failed him, Ali said "Now it's my turn," came out of his protective position, and punched furiously.[13] Foreman went down. The referee counted to nine before the bell rang to end the round. But Foreman was not getting up anyway. The referee stopped the fight. Ali had accomplished what so many other champions, including Jack Johnson and Joe Louis, had failed to do. He had won the belt a second time. He was, once again, heavyweight champion of the world.

Foreman was so disappointed with himself for losing that he took a year off to rethink his career. He then returned to the ring and defeated a number of rivals in devastating fashion before losing a second fight to Jimmy Young in 1977. After the second loss, Foreman, like Ali, underwent a religious conversion and was ordained a Baptist minister. Suddenly his old meanness was replaced with a winning smile. He returned to the ring in the mid-1980s in the unfamiliar role of crowd favorite and continued to fight well through the 1990s, regaining the belt briefly as a forty-five-year-old in 1994. But he would never fight another battle as big as the Rumble in the Jungle. "[Ali] won fair and square," Foreman would say in later years. "And now I'm just proud to be a part of the Ali legend."[14]

Indeed, Ali's victory during the Rumble in the Jungle shocked the world. *Ring* magazine, which had refused to give Ali an award years earlier after his conversion and his Vietnam protests, named Ali its "Fighter of the Year." *Sports Illustrated* named him "Sportsman of the Year." He won the Hickock Belt as the United States' best athlete. On December 10, 1974, President Gerald Ford hosted Ali at the White House, a sure sign that the nation had changed its opinion both of Ali and of the Vietnam War. "It was like the whole history of 'I ain't got no quarrel with them Vietcong' and the hatred and ugliness had been washed away," said writer Jerry Izenberg.[15]

Twenty minutes after Ali knocked Foreman down, the threatening clouds over Kinshasa finally let loose a powerful rainstorm. Ignoring the storm, young and old citizens of Zaire lined the roads that Ali traveled back to Mobutu's compound in N'Sele. They continued the chant, "Ali, bomaye!"

Three hours after winning the heavyweight championship for a second time, three hours after the most important victory of his life, reporters found Ali at the N'Sele compound, playing with some children from the surrounding area. He was performing magic tricks, and the children were delighted.

7

Decline

Elijah Muhammad died suddenly on February 25, 1975, four months after Ali regained the heavyweight crown. Before he died, Elijah selected his oldest son, Wallace Muhammad, to succeed him as the head of the Nation of Islam. In some ways, it was an odd choice for Elijah to make. Wallace had never been his favorite son, at least not publicly. During the disputes with Malcolm X in the early 1960s, Wallace sided with Malcolm against his father, and was excommunicated. Even now, ten years later, he was faithful to orthodox Islamic teachings. So few members of the Nation were surprised when Wallace immediately engineered plans to redirect the Nation and its policies. First he changed the name of the Nation of Islam to "The World Community of Al-Islam in the West." Then he refuted his father's controversial doctrines about black superiority, the inherent evil of white people, the story of Yacub, of W. D. Fard, and even of

Elijah Muhammad (lower right) listening as Ali addresses a Black Muslim convention. When Elijah died, he was succeeded as leader of the Nation of Islam by his son Wallace.

Elijah's role as the messenger of Allah. In the end, Wallace fulfilled Malcolm X's final dream: He created a community of worshipers who believed in the same principles as the rest of the world's Islamic population.

For Ali, who had been quietly moving away from Elijah's teachings for years, Wallace's reforms were a welcome change. "[Wallace] showed that color don't matter," Ali said years later. "He taught that we're responsible for our own lives and it's no good to blame our problems on other people. And that sounded right to me so I followed Wallace, but not everyone in the Nation felt that way."[1] Among the ministers who disagreed with Wallace's reforms was the head of the Nation's Boston Temple, Louis Farrakhan. A former calypso singer named Gene Walcott, Farrakhan discovered Elijah's teachings in the mid-1950s and changed his name first to Louis X. As a fiery preacher with controversial views about the inadequacy of integration, Farrakhan resurrected the old-style Nation of Islam in 1977. But Ali took the path outlined by Wallace and, with time, would become a devout orthodox Muslim just as his friend Malcolm X had in the year before his death.

Ali took five months off to recover from his grueling bout with Foreman, and his nearly suicidal rope-a-dope strategy. He did not train very hard during this period. His next opponent, Chuck Wepner, a thirty-five-year-old liquor salesman from Bayonne, New Jersey, was supposed to be an easy win for Ali, and the champion seemed to forget the lessons he had learned after the first fight with Ken Norton. "I won't suffer for Wepner," Ali announced when reporters suggested he was out of shape. "I want to fight for ten more years, and so I can't go all out for every fight. This sucker is a cinch."[2] Indeed Wepner, known as "The Bayonne Bleeder" for his tendency to get cut in the ring, proved to be a cinch. But in round nine, with Ali firmly in command of the fight, Wepner stepped on Ali's foot by accident and knocked the champion to the canvas—not a true knockdown—but Tony Perez, the same referee who mistakenly saved Joe Frazier from a knockdown during the second Ali-Frazier contest, began the count anyway. Perez's count angered Ali, and the champion released his anger on Wepner. "Take this one," he said as he punched Wepner's bloodied eyes. "Here's another."[3] Critics would once again charge Ali with brutally beating his opponent, just as he had done to Floyd Patterson and Ernie Terrell. Perez called off the fight in the fifteenth round, leaving Wepner to nurse his swollen eyes and broken nose. Afterward, Ali made unfounded accusations about Perez, saying he allowed Wepner to use rabbit punches and had perhaps taken money from gangsters to stop Ali's fight against Frazier in the second round. Perez sued Ali for libel and asked for a $20-million settlement in district court. But Perez was up against a national hero and ultimately lost the case. Later, Ali and Perez reconciled their differences.

Perhaps the only positive result of the Wepner fight was that it inspired a young, struggling actor named Sylvester Stallone, who watched the fight on closed-circuit TV. Impressed by Wepner's eagerness to take on the heavyweight champion, and shocked to see Wepner knock the great Ali down, Stallone began work on a movie script about a poor, struggling boxer's shot at the title—Chuck Wepner became the inspiration for "Rocky Balboa," one of the most beloved characters in movie history.

Controversy once again followed Ali after the Wepner fight. Although he was often generous—sometimes too generous for his own good—and kind to his friends, and although the people of the United States once again accepted him as a worthy champion, Ali was far from perfect. As he had shown in the Patterson, Terrell, and Wepner matches, he was vicious when he lost his temper. As he had demonstrated while training with Archie Moore—and then with every other trainer, manager, and advisor who disagreed with him—he could be stubborn and demanding. But Ali's worst flaws were the ones confined to his home life. Though a proud father with a growing family by 1975, Ali did not often stay in one place long enough to be a regular presence in their daily lives. Constantly in training, or traveling, or promoting fights, or speaking for his religion, or speaking out against war, or surrounded by his entourage, he never learned to change diapers or fill a baby's bottle. But worst of all, he was not a faithful husband. On the road to his fights and countless public appearances, he often spent time with women other than his wife Belinda, despite Islamic prohibitions against extramarital affairs. In 1975, his weakness finally became a topic of public discussion.

During the long days in Zaire, Ali had met a woman named Veronica Porche, a poster-girl for the Rumble in the Jungle promotions. She was a beautiful woman with an appreciation for fine clothes and jewelry, as fashionable as Belinda was religious. She stayed with Ali at Mobutu's compound in the days leading up to the fight. During the summer of 1975, after fighting Wepner, Ron Lyle, and Joe Bugner for the second time (three fights in five months), Ali was looking for an opportunity to spend time away from Belinda and with his new love. So he scheduled a fight in Manila, the largest city in the Philippines, against his old opponent Joe Frazier. Looking for one more shot at regaining his belt, and one more chance to silence Ali, Frazier was enthusiastic about the fight. But since Frazier's career was waning by 1975, Ali only

Ali at the weigh-in before facing Joe Frazier in Manila

signed on because he could hide away with Veronica while he trained in Manila, and because the Filipino president, dictator Ferdinand Marcos, asked Ali to fight in the Philippines for the publicity the fight would generate.

In preparation for the fight, scheduled for October 1 in Quezon City just outside of Manila, Ali trained hard and ridiculed Frazier even harder. "Joe Frazier is completely washed up," he said. "This is a pitiful fight. He ain't nothin' but a punchin' bag."[4] He told the press that Frazier was stupid, and even made fun of Frazier's dark complexion, calling him "the Gorilla." Frazier, who was not a skilled speaker like Ali, became even more frustrated and angry as the fight approached, and once again channeled his anger into his training sessions. But while Frazier prepared for the fight, Ali's private life was falling apart. During a banquet, Ferdinand Marcos referred to Veronica as Ali's wife, and Ali did not correct him. When word of Ali's mistake reached Belinda in the States, she boarded an airplane bound for Manila, ready to confront her unfaithful husband. After a brief, loud argument with Ali in his hotel room, she got back on a plane, returned to the United States, and immediately filed for divorce. Suddenly the world knew about Ali's troubles.

Against this background of personal anguish, Ali fought in what many experts consider to be the greatest boxing match of all time. It was as warm as 110° F (43° C) under the lights in the Philippines Coliseum on the humid night of September 30. Once again, Ali was fighting in the middle of the night so that audiences in the United States could watch the fight live. Frazier entered the ring first, a lean 215 pounds (97.5 kg). Then the thirty-three-year-old champion entered, heavy at 224 pounds (101.6 kg). As the ring announcer made his introductions, Ali marched to the center of the ring, swooped up the trophy that Marcos would be awarding to the winner of the fight, and carried it back to his corner. The crowd laughed and booed simultaneously, and Ali pretended to cry about their reaction. It was a typical Ali performance, playing to the crowd, staying loose. But when the bell finally rang to begin the action, Ali was all business.

He tried to knock out Frazier early in the round, taunting him, pulling his head down as he did in their second fight, throwing furious jabs at Frazier's face. He continued his onslaught in the second round, to surprisingly little effect. Frazier was ready for a long battle. In the third round, Ali waved Frazier on and fell back against the ropes—resurrecting the rope-a-dope strategy. In the fourth round, as Frazier pounded at his body, Ali led the crowd in the cheer "A-li, A-li." But in the fifth, Frazier sent a blistering punch to Ali's face, stunned him, and won his first round. Ali tried dancing in the sixth, but he was no longer quick enough to escape Frazier's attack. The tide had turned. By the seventh round, the two men were fighting an even match. In the eighth, Ali rallied and scored heavy blows to Frazier's head, but Frazier recovered and had Ali staggering at the end of the round. In the ninth and tenth rounds, they continued to hammer away at each other. Before the start of the eleventh, Ali was almost ready to quit, wounded after Frazier's attack and baking in the intense heat under the Coliseum lights. "I think this is what dying is like," he whispered to his cornermen.[5] He returned to the rope-a-dope strategy to conserve energy. In round twelve, he unleashed a desperate flurry of punches, more like slaps now, connecting with many of them. Frazier's face was swollen; his eyes were almost closed. In the thirteenth round, it was obvious that Frazier could no longer see Ali's fists as they whipped at his head. Frazier's manager, Eddie Futch, decided that he had seen enough. He would not let his fighter get off the corner stool for the fourteenth round. "Sit down, son, it's all over," Futch said to his brave fighter, who nearly beat the world champion when everyone thought he was washed up. "No one will ever forget what you did here today."[6]

Ali did not raise his arms in victory after Futch stopped the fight. He did not shout "I'm the greatest!" Instead, as the press and the entourage flooded the ring, Ali sat on his corner stool, his head sagging low, hurt and exhausted from the ordeal. A television reporter finally worked his way over to Ali and asked what he thought about Joe Frazier now. "He is the greatest fighter of all times next to me," Ali gasped. Asked about his future as a boxer, he responded, "This is too painful. It's too much work. Might have a heart attack or something. I want to get out while I'm on top."[7] Ali took nearly 440 punches during the fight that will forever be known as "The Thrilla in Manila." He won the fight, but the victory took a terrible toll on his body.

After the fight, in the dressing rooms, Ali called to Frazier's son Marvis. "Tell your dad the things I said I really didn't mean." After the incredible battle, Ali wanted Frazier to know that the harsh words he had directed at him were for the benefit of the fight promotion and did not represent what he truly believed.

"He should come to me, son," Frazier responded when he heard what Ali said. "He should say it to my face."[8] For twenty years following their third fight, Frazier would continue the rivalry, belittling Ali at every opportunity just as Ali had belittled him throughout the early 1970s. Only in early 1997, twenty-two years after their last meeting in the ring, would Frazier once again extend his friendship to Ali.

Victories in the Rumble in the Jungle and the Thrilla in Manila sealed Ali's status as a boxing legend. In 1976, Ali and Frazier shared "Fighter of the Year" honors for their performance in the Philippines, and both were now ranked among the top ten greatest fighters of all time by boxing experts. But Ali was at the top of the list; as he had been claiming for twenty years, he was now officially "The Greatest of All Times," an icon beyond his sport and beyond his native land. In May 1976, he was invited to a filming of the CBS television program "Face the Nation," which normally interviewed political figures and world leaders. During the show, he was asked to defend his stand on Vietnam and his religious beliefs. Ali used the show as an opportunity to announce his changing views about race relations in the United States. "Wallace Muhammad is on time," he said. "He's teaching us it's not the color of the physical body that makes a man a devil. God looks at our minds and our actions and our deeds."[9] But while Ali was defending Wallace on television, he was trying to pacify the new leader of the Nation in private. Like his father, Wallace objected to Ali's insistence that he continue his boxing career. He objected to the brutality of the sport, feared for Ali's health, and was angry about Ali's marital difficulties, which were becoming more public every day. Ali's friends would continue to be concerned about these aspects of his life for years to come.

On February 20, 1976, Ali fought the champion of Belgium, Jean-Pierre Coopman. Hoping to generate some interest in the fight, Ali called Coopman "The Lion of Flanders." But the Lion refused to roar: Grateful for the opportunity to fight against the Champ, Coopman hugged and kissed Ali during pre-fight interviews and drank champagne between rounds of the five-round bout. Ali won easily.

But in the next fight, it became apparent that his boxing skills were declining. Jimmy Young, the 230-pound (104.3-kg) fighter who had defeated George Foreman a month earlier, took Ali the distance. The Champ managed to squeeze out a victory by decision, but boxing fans were complaining again that Ali's reputation, and not his performance, was the deciding factor. It was the same criticism he had faced after the Doug Jones fight in 1963, only this time Ali's skills were obviously eroding. He silenced the critics for a short time when he took on Richard Dunn in Munich and knocked him down five times in five rounds. But after the Thrilla, Muhammad Ali was a different fighter, and it was only a matter of time before a young, skilled boxer would come along to take his belt.

Bad decision-making and Ali's stubborn refusal to heed the advice of the more concerned members of his entourage made the situation worse. In June, Ali faced a Japanese professional wrestler for what he called "the martial arts championship of the world." Originally arranged as a multimillion-dollar publicity stunt to showcase Ali's skills and charm in Tokyo, the bout was arranged for wrestler Antonio Inoki to cheat his way to victory, giving Ali an opportunity to shout and scream about being tricked. But either Ali refused to fool the public, or Inoki's manager refused to let his wrestler enter a fixed match.[10] Either way, Inoki approached the bout as a real fight. He stayed low to the mat and kicked at Ali's legs for fifteen rounds. Ali left the ring with horribly bruised legs, and the fight was called a draw. From Tokyo, he went on to Manila and Korea for fight exhibitions but ended up in a U.S. hospital for treatment on the blood clots and muscle damage he received during the Inoki fiasco.

Three months later he was back in the ring against Ken Norton, one of his most dangerous rivals. The fight took place in Yankee Stadium during a New York City police strike that left the stadium without heavy security. Before a rowdy, dangerous crowd, the fighters faced off for the third time in their careers. Ali lost the early rounds but came back to even the fight going into the fifteenth round. Norton, who believed he was comfortably in the lead, did not attack during the last round, giving Ali the opportunity to win the round and the fight. The crowd booed the decision as the fighters left the ring. Reporters accused the judges of giving Ali a victory he did not deserve. Even Norton said publicly that he had been robbed.

Ali and Ken Norton battling it out at Yankee Stadium in 1976

Ali's boxing career was quite obviously in decline by the end of 1976, and he took eight months off after the Norton fight. In May of 1977, he fought a young boxer named Alfredo Evangelista in Spain. Though a professional for only nineteen months, Evangelista survived the full fifteen rounds. It was a fight the young Cassius Clay, or even the young Ali, would have ended in four rounds.

Following the fight, Ali and Belinda settled their divorce agreement, and on June 19, he married Veronica, with whom he already had a ten-month-old baby girl named Hana. Ali invited Howard Bingham to accompany him and Veronica on their honeymoon in Hawaii. But he had grown so used to crowds and attention that he was bored—even with Bingham to entertain him—and called the honeymoon off after three days. He went straight back to the gym to train for his upcoming September 29 bout against heavy-puncher Earnie Shavers. The Shavers fight was yet another indication that Ali was nearing the end of his career. Only a late, fifteenth-round onslaught preserved his title.

The most shocking thing about Ali's fights after the brutal Thrilla was that he actually looked ill. Once the great poet of the ring, Ali's speech was slurred. His reflexes were no longer as sharp as they had been. His legs looked heavy and slow. After the Shavers fight, Teddy Brenner, head of Madison Square Garden boxing, held a press conference to announce that he would no longer sign contracts allowing Ali to fight in boxing's most important arena. The New York State Athletic Commission then sponsored a physical examination. Dr. Frank Guardino found evidence of kidney damage and blood in Ali's urine. Both Guardino and Ferdie Pacheco advised Ali to quit boxing to preserve his health. Ali refused. In protest, Pacheco quit the entourage.

As Ali's body was failing him, he was reaching new levels of popularity and public exposure. In 1975, his autobiography, *The Greatest*, was published by Random House. In truth, Ali did only a small amount of work on the book. His cowriter, Richard Durham, was an editor of *Muhammad Speaks*, a publication of the Nation of Islam. His editor was Toni Morrison, the future Nobel Prize–winning novelist. Durham and Morrison collaborated on most of the text, which included, among other tall tales, the famous story of Ali's lost gold medal. In addition to the book, Ali put the finishing touches on his biographical movie, *The Greatest*, with Columbia Pictures. Ali starred as himself and was backed by a prestigious supporting cast—actors Robert Duvall, Paul

Winfield, and James Earl Jones. Even DC Comics grabbed a piece of the action when they pitted Ali against their most popular superhero in "Superman vs. Muhammad Ali: The Fight to Save Earth from Star-Warriors."

Ali's opponents in real life were not supermen however. At the beginning of 1978, Ali was getting ready to fight Leon Spinks, a newcomer to the professional ranks. Spinks grew up in a low-income housing project in St. Louis. Like Ken Norton, he escaped the ghetto by joining the Marines. Spinks went on to win the gold medal at the 1976 Olympics. Before signing on to fight Ali, he fought only seven bouts, including six victories over bad fighters and a draw. Ali did very little to promote the fight. He announced that a victory over Spinks would give him a victory over every active Olympic gold medal-winner (Floyd Patterson, Joe Frazier, George Foreman, and Leon Spinks). He called Spinks "Goofy" and "Dracula" because the fighter was missing his front teeth. But that was all. Spinks was so young and unskilled that there was almost nothing for Ali to say. Most boxing experts agreed that Spinks did not belong in the same ring with Ali. More important, however, Ali did not even train. He set himself up for disaster. Spinks tore a rib-cage muscle while training and was having problems lifting his right arm. But given Ali's poor condition at fight time, and the slow decline of his ability, he could not even stand up to an injured Spinks. He tried the rope-a-dope strategy, but the younger Spinks never tired. So on February 15, 1978, in Las Vegas, Nevada, Muhammad Ali lost his championship belt for the first time in the ring.

After the fight, Ali sat on a massage table in the dressing room and fielded questions from the press. Reporters and some members of the entourage tried to cheer him up, telling him that the judges made a bad decision. "Shut up! I lost!" Ali shouted.[11] To another re-

Leon Spinks won a fifteen-round decision against Ali when they met in Las Vegas in 1978.

porter who insisted on calling him "Champ" after the loss, Ali said "You don't have to call me champ to be my friend."[12] He tried to be gracious in defeat, as he had been when he lost to Frazier in the Fight of the Century. But without the belt, he was hungry again. Even when Dundee suggested that Ali retire, the fighter would not listen. The night after the fight, unable to sleep, Ali got out of bed and laced up his sneakers. Still hurting from the Spinks fight, he went outside at two o'clock in the morning for a long jog, saying to himself as he ran, "Gotta get my title back."[13]

Counting on Ali's popularity to produce another huge box office draw and more money, Spinks granted Ali a rematch. The fight was scheduled for September 15 so Ali had some time to recover from the first matchup, and also to embark on a goodwill tour through Asia and the Soviet Union. In the Soviet Union, he met with Premier Leonid Brezhnev, calling himself the "unofficial ambassador for peace with the United States." With U.S.-Soviet tensions running high through the 1970s and early 1980s, Brezhnev was considered an enemy in the United States. To his surprise, Ali found the premier personable, even friendly. "This is a great honor for a Negro from America," he told reporters. "I love the food in America, the TV, the movies, the highways and cars, the flag and the president. And I also love the truth."[14] The truth, for Ali, was that the Soviet Union and the United States were trapped in a misunderstanding. Both nations wanted peace, he believed, and peace was possible if the leaders of both nations would meet only the way he and Brezhnev had met.

While Ali was traveling across Asia, Spinks was taking advantage of his newfound fame. He refused to train, discovered big city party life, and was even arrested for cocaine possession. He was out of control by the late summer. More than 63,000 people crowded into the Superdome in New Orleans to see the match on September 15, breaking every ticket record in history. The fight attracted ABC's second-largest television audience ever. Ali was slow-footed and weak in the ring, but Spinks fought so foolishly that he had to lose. Spinks's cornermen argued over strategy, and his trainer, George Benton, left the arena in frustration. Ali won the fifteen-round decision and the championship for an unprecedented third time (Evander Holyfield would tie Ali's record in 1996).

President Jimmy Carter called Ali to congratulate him after his victory. Carter told Ali that he watched the fight at Camp David with the president of Egypt, Anwar Sadat, and the prime minister of Israel, Menachem Begin. There the three men were hammering out the details of a historic Middle East peace settlement. Perhaps it was the president's message or perhaps it was his experience in the Soviet Union that inspired Ali's announcement on June 26, 1979: Ten months after regaining the heavyweight title, Ali retired from boxing. He planned to devote the rest of his life to the cause of peace. "I'm getting out of boxing," he said. "Boxing was the dressing room, a preliminary to the big fight—for humanity, racial justice, freedom and human rights. . . ."[15]

8

Peace

Ali, Veronica, and their daughters Hana and Laila moved to Los Angeles after Ali announced his retirement. The Champ had just completed his part in the filming of a television miniseries called *Freedom Road* with actor Kris Kristofferson, and thought he was ready for the Hollywood lifestyle. He was wrong. Even though he was the top money-making boxer of all time, he was a terrible money manager. His biggest problem, as the Nation of Islam suggested years earlier, was that he was too generous. He was constantly giving money to charities, to hitch-hikers, to the homeless, to neighborhood children, to anyone who asked. His entourage grew enormously over the years, and he created as many paying positions as there were people. And now with Ali's approval, Veronica was buying art works and other luxuries for the new house with little concern for their dwindling savings.

Then there was the problem of his awful business sense. Whenever a member of the entourage asked him to endorse a product, support a business, or make a public appearance, Ali agreed. Many of the business deals he entered were either failures or scams. In 1978, a group of bankers and accountants offered Ali their services, free of charge, so that he could arrange his finances sensibly and prepare for the future. But when members of the old boxing entourage continued to influence Ali's decisions, at one point involving him in an oil company backed by Libyan dictator Muammar al-Qaddafi, the bankers ended their relationship with him.

By early 1980, Ali's financial situation was rapidly deteriorating. In addition, he was restless with his new, quiet life at home with Veronica. He grew uncomfortable watching other boxers battle for the title he held for so long, and haunted by members of the entourage who were out of work now that he was no longer boxing. He once again looked to the boxing ring as the only place where he could be happy. On March 5, he announced his decision to break his retirement for one more shot at the title, against the new World Boxing Association champion John Tate. Tate lost shortly after Ali's announcement, however, so Ali decided to take on the new heavyweight champion of the world, Larry Holmes, instead. In addition to the glory of winning the belt a fourth time, Ali would receive a much-needed $8 million for the fight.

Ali and Holmes knew and respected each other long before their fight on October 2, 1980, in Las Vegas. Holmes had been Ali's sparring partner for three years at Deer Lake in the mid-1970s. He had even traveled to Zaire for the Rumble in the Jungle, but he became homesick in N'Sele and returned to the States before the fight. When Ali retired in 1979, Holmes fought and won a series of bouts and emerged as the undisputed heavyweight champion. He was a talented, sound boxer. But the public wanted a champion as flamboyant as the one they lost, and the quiet, businesslike Holmes could not be that champion. He could handle himself in the ring, however, so he accepted Ali's challenge. Even though Ali was a mere shadow of the boxer he once had been, he was still a great self-promoter, and Holmes nearly fell victim to his pre-fight hype. As Holmes would later recall, "He was always saying, 'Hey, I told you with Sonny Liston; I told you with George Foreman.' And if you listened, you'd believe him. You'd say, 'What the hell am I fighting this guy for?' So it was rough for me to sleep at night. I was fighting Muhammad Ali."[1]

Holmes had nothing to worry about. Ali's physical condition was worse than anyone could have expected. Before training, he ballooned to 250 pounds (113.4 kg). His reflexes were terrible, and he was hard to understand when he spoke. Some observers assumed that he was "punch drunk," that years of boxing had resulted in brain and nerve damage, a common ailment among aging boxers. Responding to public concern, the Nevada State Athletic Commission sponsored a two-day examination for Ali at the Mayo Clinic in Rochester, Minnesota. After putting Ali through a battery of tests, the doctors at the clinic announced that the Champ had passed his examination. Surprisingly, they made this announcement after mentioning that Ali felt tingling in his hands, that his agility had decreased measurably, and that he could not touch his finger to his nose without difficulty.[2] After the Mayo exam, Herbert Muhammad's doctor, Charles Williams, took over Ali's case. Williams diagnosed Ali's ailment as a thyroid condition mixed with hypoglycemia, or low blood sugar, and prescribed a number of hormones to help balance his body chemicals. To Ali's de-

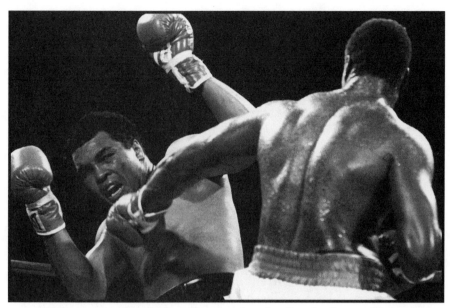

Ali was on the decline by the time he fought Larry Holmes in October 1980.

light, the medicines reduced his weight to 217 pounds (98.43 kg) by the day of the fight. He looked better than he had in years. But the hormones also weakened him.

No one tried to prevent the fight, although Ali looked terrible in his sparring sessions. Even Dundee supported the decision to go on. "He's not of this earth," the trainer said. "My guy is from outer space. He ain't human. He will win."[3] But the man "from outer space" was now thirty-eight years old and physically unstable. And Dundee did not know about the hormones Ali had been taking. Ali entered the ring quietly on October 2. Holmes was also quiet, and physically fit at 211 pounds (95.7 kg). From the opening bell he carried the fight, dominating his childhood hero. Then Holmes backed away and tried not to knock Ali down, and not to embarrass him before the world. Ali did not win a single round and landed only ten solid punches in ten rounds. At times, Holmes held him up and waited for the referee to stop the fight. Finally, before the eleventh round, Herbert Muhammad and Angelo Dundee threw in the towel. Ali could not pull off another miracle.

Holmes cried after the fight, sad to have beaten his hero so badly. Ali, who had just experienced the worst defeat of his career, actually had to console the winner. When Holmes addressed the press, he graciously put Ali's defeat in perspective: "He's one hell of an athlete, one hell of a man. Even trying to win a fourth title is one hell of an accomplishment."[4] Four days after the fight, Ali was taken to UCLA Medical Center. His body had not recovered from the fight and his friends were worried that something was seriously wrong. After running a series of tests, doctors at UCLA determined that the thyroid and hypoglycemia medications Ali had been taking were putting him in serious danger. Among other things, the hormones caused heat stroke, weakness, fatigue, uncontrolled weight loss, and dehydration. But this news gave Ali hope: He now believed that the drugs were responsible for his loss against Holmes, and held out the hope for one more miraculous comeback.

While Ali was concentrating on the Holmes fight, he was once again a topic of discussion in the White House. The 1980 Summer Olympics were scheduled to take place in Moscow, but after the Soviet Union invaded the neighboring nation of Afghanistan in 1979, President Carter and Congress supported a boycott of the games. Right after the Holmes fight, while Ali was on a goodwill tour through India, Carter contacted him and asked him to head a diplomatic mission to Africa to encourage

African support for the U.S. boycott. Carter was hoping to capitalize on Ali's popularity on the African continent, particularly after the legendary Rumble in the Jungle. Ali, flattered to be offered such an important mission, accepted Carter's offer. On February 2, 1980, he embarked on a multi-nation tour, meeting with mid-level officials in Tanzania, Kenya, Nairobi, Nigeria, Liberia, and Senegal. The people of Africa welcomed Ali warmly, but the leaders were offended that Carter had sent an athlete to do a diplomat's job. In addition, the African leaders had not forgotten the United States' refusal to support a boycott of the 1976 Olympics in protest of South Africa's policy of apartheid (the legalized oppression of the nation's black majority). And many of them actually supported and were backed by the Soviet Union. Shoved into a serious political conflict, and angry about the cool reception he received from African leaders, Ali continued to explain the Carter administration's position on the boycott. But he also complained that he was traveling "around the world to take the whupping over American policies."[5] His mission was a failure.

With memories of the Africa fiasco, the Holmes fight, and even the first Spinks fight still fresh in his mind, Ali decided that he was tired of defeat and wanted one more victory in the ring so that he could finally retire on a positive note. Most people who knew Ali, and were concerned about his physical deterioration, refused to honor his request for a final fight. But a promoter named James Cornelius—a convicted thief—arranged a fight to give both Ali and himself one more payday. Ali's opponent was Trevor Berbick, a boxer from the Bahamas. The fight was scheduled for ten rounds and set for December 11, 1981, on the Bahamian island of Nassau. It would be an unfortunate send-off for a great champion. Bahamian officials only approved two pairs of boxing gloves for all

117

the fights on the December 11 card. So by the time Ali laced up, the gloves were heavy with the sweat of other boxers. As if that were not bad enough, ringside officials used a cowbell to announce the beginning and the end of each round. Worst of all, the fight was boring. Berbick beat Ali soundly in all ten rounds. It was a humiliating defeat but Ali spoke humbly at the post-fight press conference. "After the Holmes fight," he said, "I had excuses. No excuses this time. I was in shape, my weight was right. Berbick was just stronger, he was hard to hit."[6] There were no doubts now, Ali's boxing career was officially over. Veteran sportswriter Ed Schuyler spoke for everyone present at the press conference, and for Ali's fans around the world, when he stood and said, "Muhammad, thank you. You gave us a hell of a ride."[7]

After the Berbick fight, Ali finally came to terms with his life away from the boxing ring. Early on, he missed the spotlight, the entourage, the media attention. But he did not rush into a new occupation. He turned down a series of job offers, including a position as a television sportscaster and a $10-million deal to work for a U.S. oil company in the Middle East. He pursued his humanitarian interests and, increasingly, looked to his Muslim faith for strength and guidance. Slowly, he cleaned up his personal life and stopped chasing women, though his ailments ensured that he could no longer live a fast lifestyle. And he once again participated in civil rights negotiations, encouraging America to move beyond the violence of the 1960s and 1970s, and the divisions that he once symbolized. "When I was young," he would say, "I fol-

Over the years, Muhammad Ali has turned to his religion for answers. As part of his daily routine, he faces East and kneels to pray.

lowed a teaching that disrespected other people and said that white people were 'devils.' I was wrong. Color does not make a man a devil. It's the heart and soul and mind that count."[8] In the end, Ali created his own unique occupation. He became an ambassador of Islam, carrying his message of peace around the world.

Ali's failing health was a major obstacle to his new pursuits, however. By 1984, his hands had begun to tremble, and he was often overcome with fatigue. In September of that year, he entered Columbia-Presbyterian Medical Center in Manhattan for a thorough examination. After years of speculation, doctors finally determined that Ali suffered from Parkinson's syndrome.

Unlike Parkinson's *disease*, which is hereditary, the syndrome is caused by brain trauma, probably the result of the thousands of punches Ali received in his long career—particularly during the rope-a-dope years. After so many blows to the head, certain brain cells begin to degenerate and die. Although the syndrome does not affect his intelligence or threaten his life, it does result in obvious, visible symptoms: a shuffling walk, trembling hands, a mask-like face, and slurred speech.

Ali's doctors have prescribed a series of medicines that improve his appearance, if he takes them on a regular basis. But Ali often ignores the doctors' advice and, as a result, does not always look as healthy as he could. The syndrome is the price he pays for twenty-five years of fantastic showmanship, of legendary victories, and of the tremendous risks he took with his body. Ali's friends are sometimes disheartened by his condition. His father, Cash, once remarked, "Told him to quit boxin'. Shoulda made movies. He was bigger than anybody. Prettier, too, and smarter. I met Elvis—all pimply-faced, ugly next to Ali. Not smart, either."[9] Ali does not look at his affliction as a boxing injury, however. As in many other aspects of his life since boxing, he chooses to find spiritual value in his changed appearance. "I know why this happened," he says. "God is showing me, and showing *you* that I'm just a man, just like everybody else."[10]

Of course, even if he is "just a man," Ali remains an amazingly influential public figure. In November of 1990, for instance, while the United States and Iraq were gearing up for the Persian Gulf War, Ali met with Saddam Hussein in an attempt to persuade the Iraqi leader to release his six hundred U.S., British, and Japanese hostages. At a time when U.S. diplomats were failing to make any progress in the hostage crisis, Hussein agreed to release fifteen U.S. citizens out of respect for Ali.

120

But as a famously generous public figure, Ali is always in danger of being tricked by untrustworthy schemers. Impostors have used his name to influence decisions in the U.S. Senate. Businessmen have used his name to endorse faulty products. Even Herbert Muhammad has used his name in money-making schemes. To help Ali with his finances, his business decisions, and his struggle with Parkinson's syndrome, his old neighbor Lonnie Williams, who once lived in the house next to the Clay family's Louisville residence, quit her job and joined Ali in Los Angeles. Lonnie's mother was Odessa Clay's best friend. Thirteen years younger than the Champ, she was a little girl when the handsome Olympian, Cassius Clay, would visit his mother in Louisville and play with all of the children on the block. As she grew up, attending Vanderbuilt University and then the University of Louisville business school, she tracked Ali's progress through the boxing world. In 1982, when Ali was depressed about retirement and losing his early battles with Parkinson's, Lonnie ran to him. Under Ali's guidance, she converted to Islam and the two developed a strong friendship. Then, in the summer of 1986, his marriage with Veronica fell apart. By the end of the year, Ali had divorced Veronica and married Lonnie.

With Lonnie's support, Ali emerged from the difficult transition to retirement and, by the late 1980s, was once again a powerful presence in the media. In 1987, he was unanimously inducted into *Ring* magazine's Hall of Fame, one of the most important honors a boxer can receive.[11] In 1992, a large group of friends and admirers threw Ali a fiftieth birthday party, which was broadcast on national television. A year later, he fulfilled his lifelong dream of visiting South Africa—a nation that had finally emerged from the bonds of apartheid. As a hero of the U.S. civil rights struggle, he was greeted by Nelson Mandela and Oliver Tambo, the heroes of the South African freedom movement. In 1994, *Sports Illustrated* honored him as the most important sports figure of the last forty years. Reporter William Nack wrote the magazine's official assessment of Ali's career:

> *Ali fought professionally for more than 20 years, from 1960 to 1981, and his life was so brassy and daring, so filled with wonders and adventure, and so enlarged by the magic of his personality and the play of his mind that no one remotely like him has ever been seen on the sporting scene.*[12]

Ali enjoyed a bit of Hollywood succcess when a 1996 documentary recounting the Rumble in the Jungle and entitled *When We Were Kings* won an Academy Award. At the Oscar ceremonies, Ali and George Foreman joined director Leon Gast on stage, in front of a worldwide television audience, to celebrate the legendary bout they had fought more than twenty years earlier.

But the highlight of Ali's later career as a public figure has been his dramatic torch-lighting at the 1996 Olympics. With 3.5 billion people watching on television, the wounded champion stood as a symbol of strength and courage, no longer ashamed of his imperfect appearance. As Lonnie described later, even Ali was amazed by the crowd's response and by his own response to the honor: "He just sat in a chair in his hotel room with the torch. He kept turning it in his hands and looking at it. . . . I think it gave him new courage."[13]

Although he has received countless awards for his work in the ring and in the political forum, Ali has also experienced his share of sadness in these years. His friend Drew "Bundini" Brown died in 1988. His cook and confidante, Lana Shabazz, died in 1990, as did his father Cassius Sr. And the hardest blow came in August 1994,

Ali was hit hard by the death of his parents. Cassius and Odessa Clay are shown here in 1965, prior to their son's bout against Sonny Liston.

when his seventy-seven-year-old mother, Odessa Lee Grady Clay, died of heart failure in a nursing home. Ali slipped into a mild depression after his mother's death, emerging months later to continue his public role as the world's goodwill ambassador.

Today Ali signs a thousand Islamic pamphlets a day and passes them out on his travels. Even with his disabilities, he travels 275 days a year, visiting major cities and small villages around the world. Although he does not speak nearly as much as he did in his "Louisville Lip" days—he does not like what Parkinson's syndrome has done to his voice—he draws huge crowds with every public appearance, even when he ducks into McDonald's

Ali enjoyed spending time with his children and is shown here with three of his daughters at Deer Lake in 1975.

for a cup of coffee. But unlike other public figures, Ali encourages the crowds, believing that his presence can make a difference to people who need friends and support: "When I move back to [Louisville], gowna get me a place, a coffee shop, where I can give away free coffee and donuts and people can just sit and talk, people of all races, and I can go and talk to people."[14]

He now lives at Ali Farms in Berrien Springs, Michigan, but will soon return to Louisville to promote his newest venture, the Ali Center. To be completed in 2001, the museum will trace the major events of his life: his career in the ring, his role as a civil rights and antiwar activist, and his Islamic faith. For now, however, Ali continues to travel and has taken a more active role as the head of a large family. He has nine children: Maryum, Rasheeda, Jamillah, and Muhammad Jr. from his marriage to Belinda; Hana and Laila from his marriage to Veronica; Miya and Khaliah from two other relationships; and a young son named Asaad Amin, which means "Son of the Lion," whom he adopted with Lonnie.

Ali's children have grown up in a country vastly different from the land of Ali's youth. The civil rights movement of the 1960s changed forever the nation's basic assumptions about the way people of different races relate to one another. The antiwar protests of the Vietnam era changed forever the country's basic approach to war. And as a champion inside the ring, a participant in the civil rights and antiwar struggles, and an Islamic ambassador and humanitarian in his later years, Ali himself has changed forever the standards that the world holds for its heroes.

Source notes

Introduction

1. Thomas Hauser, *Muhammad Ali: His Life and Times* (New York: Simon & Schuster, 1991), p. 452.
2. Dave Kindred, "Atlanta Games," *The Atlanta Journal*, July 21, 1996, p. 34S.
3. Ibid., p. 34S.

Chapter 1

1. Hauser, *Muhammad Ali: His Life and Times*, p. 15.
2. Ibid., p. 15.
3. Ibid., p. 18.
4. Thomas Hauser, *Muhammad Ali: In Perspective* (San Francisco: Collins, 1996), p. 10.
5. Hauser, *Muhammad Ali: His Life and Times*, p. 20.
6. Ibid., p. 18.
7. Thomas R. Hietala, "Muhammad Ali and the Age of Bare-Knuckle Politics" in *Muhammad Ali: The People's Champ*, edited by Elliot J. Gorn (Chicago: University of Illinois Press, 1995), p. 119.
8. Hauser, *Muhammad Ali: His Life and Times*, p. 24.

9. Othello Harris, "Muhammad Ali and the Revolt of the Black Athlete," in *Muhammad Ali: The People's Champ*, edited by Elliot J. Gorn (Chicago: University of Illinois Press, 1995), p. 57.
10. Dave Kindred, "He'll Always Be the Greatest," *The Sporting News*, July 29, 1996, p. 6.
11. Hietala, p. 121.
12. Hauser, *Muhammad Ali: His Life and Times*, p. 29.

Chapter 2
1. Hauser, *Muhammad Ali: His Life and Times*, p. 33.
2. Ferdie Pacheco, *Muhammad Ali* (New York: Birch Lane, 1992), p. 17.
3. Ibid., p. 16.
4. Matt Schudel, "Past With a Punch," *Fort Lauderdale Sun-Sentinel*, October 15, 1995. p. 12.
5. Hauser, *Muhammad Ali: His Life and Times*, p. 36.
6. Ibid., p. 37.
7. Richard Polenburg, *One Nation Divisible: Class, Race, and Ethnicity in the United States Since 1938* (New York: Penguin, 1980), p. 150.
8. Hauser, *Muhammad Ali: His Life and Times*, p. 39.
9. Ibid., pp. 43.
10. Ibid., p. 49.
11. Pacheco, p. 182.
12. Hauser, *Muhammad Ali: His Life and Times*, p. 56.

Chapter 3
1. Polenburg, p. 189.
2. Randy Roberts, "The Wide World of Muhammad Ali: The Politics and Economics of Televised Boxing," in *Muhammad Ali: The People's Champ*, edited Elliot J. Gorn (Chicago: University of Illinois Press, 1995), p. 26.
3. Hauser, *Muhammad Ali: His Life and Times*, p. 63.

4. Jeffrey T. Sammons, *Beyond the Ring: The Role of Boxing in American Society* (Chicago: University of Illinois Press, 1988), p. 46.

5. Hauser, *Muhammad Ali: His Life and Times*, p. 64.

6. Davis Miller, *The Tao of Muhammad Ali* (New York: Warner, 1996), p. 15.

7. Hauser, *Muhammad Ali: His Life and Times*, p. 61.

8. Alex Haley and Malcolm X, *The Autobiography of Malcolm X* (New York: Ballantine, 1965), p. 313.

9. Pacheco, p. 69–70.

10. Ibid., pp. 71–73.

11. Ibid., p. 75.

12. Ibid., p. 78.

13. Hauser, *Muhammad Ali: His Life and Times*, p. 78.

14. David K. Wiggins, "Victory for Allah: Muhammad Ali, the Nation of Islam, and American Society," in *Muhammad Ali: The People's Champ*, ed. Elliot J. Gorn (Chicago: University of Illinois Press, 1995), p. 93.

15. Hauser, *Muhammad Ali: His Life and Times*, p. 82–83.

16. Hietala, p. 122.

17. Wiggins, p. 94.

Chapter Four

1. Haley and Malcolm X, p.335.

2. Ibid., p. 256.

3. Muhammad Ali and Thomas Hauser, *Healing: A Journal of Tolerance and Understanding* (San Francisco: Collins, 1996), p. 60.

4. Haley and Malcolm X, p.416.

5. Hauser, *Muhammad Ali: His Life and Times*, pp. 111–112.

6. Pacheco, p. 84.

7. Ibid., p. 84.

8. Ibid., pp. 85–86.
9. Hietala, p. 131.
10. Hauser, *Muhammad Ali: His Life and Times*, p. 139.
11. Ibid., p. 135.
12. Ibid., p. 141.
13. Ibid., p. 145.
14. Hietala, p. 139.
15. Jeffrey T. Sammons, *Beyond the Ring: The Role of Boxing in American Society* (Chicago: University of Illinois Press, 1988), p. 124.
16. Jeffrey T. Sammons, "Rebel with a Cause: Muhammad Ali as Sixties Protest Symbol," in *Muhammad Ali: The People's Champ*, edited by Eliot J. Gorn (Chicago: University of Illinois Press, 1995), p. 156.
17. Hauser, *Muhammad Ali: His Life and Times*, p. 155.
18. Ibid., p. 163.
19. Ibid., p. 179.
20. Sammons, *Beyond the Ring: The Role of Boxing in American Society*, p. 206.
21. Michael Oriard, "Muhammad Ali: The Hero in the Age of Mass Media," in *Muhammad Ali: The People's Champ*, edited by Eliot J. Gorn (Chicago: University of Illinois Press, 1995), p. 11.

Chapter Five

1. Hauser, *Muhammad Ali: His Life and Times*, p. 171.
2. Polenburg, p. 217.
3. Sammons, *Beyond the Ring*, p. 207.
4. Pacheco, p. 87.
5. Hietala, p. 146.
6. Hauser, *Muhammad Ali: His Life and Times*, p. 212.
7. Ibid., p. 237.
8. William Nack, "The Fight's Over, Joe," *Sports Illustrated*, September 30, 1996, p. 59.
9. Ibid., p. 59.

10. Gerald Suster, *Champions of the Ring: The Lives and Times of Boxing's Heavyweight Heroes* (London: Robson, 1992), p. 258.
11. Pacheco, p. 105.
12. Hauser, *Muhammad Ali: His Life and Times*, p. 232.
13. Ibid., p. 233.

Chapter Six
1. Wiggins, p. 102.
2. Hauser, *Muhammad Ali: His Life and Times*, p. 242.
3. Pacheco, p. 111.
4. Davis Miller, *The Tao of Muhammad Ali* (New York: Warner, 1996), p. 36.
5. Hauser, *Muhammad Ali: His Life and Times*, p. 256.
6. Ibid., p. 265.
7. Pacheco, p. 125.
8. Hauser, *Muhammad Ali: His Life and Times*, p. 266.
9. Ibid., p. 269.
10. Pacheco, p. 128.
11. Ibid., p. 129.
12. Ibid., p. 130.
13. Hauser, *Muhammad Ali: His Life and Times*, p. 275.
14. Ibid., p. 278.
15. Hauser, *Muhammad Ali: In Perspective*, p. 119.

Chapter Seven
1. Hauser, *Muhammad Ali: His Life and Times*, p. 294.
2. Peter Bonventre, "Fool's Gold," *Newsweek*, April 7, 1975, p. 59.
3. Ibid., p. 59.
4. Pacheco, p.136.
5. Ibid., p. 139.
6. Ibid., p. 141.
7. "The Thrilla in Manila" from NBC Sports Greatest Fights Ever videotape series.

8. Nack, "The Fight's Over, Joe," p. 67.
9. Wiggins, p. 108.
10. Hauser, *Muhammad Ali: His Life and Times*, p. 337.
11. Hauser, *Muhammad Ali: In Perspective*, p. 131.
12. Kenneth Denlinger, "Project-Raised Spinks Can't Wait to Travel," *The Washington Post*, February 17, 1978, p. C3.
13. Hauser, *Muhammad Ali: His Life and Times*, p. 354.
14. Kevin Klose, "Ali in Moscow," *The Washington Post*, June 20, 1978, p. A1.
15. Dave Brady, "Ali Remains Evasive on Retirement," *The Washington Post*, September 17, 1978, p. F1.

Chapter Eight
1. Hauser, *Muhammad Ali: In Perspective*, p. 133.
2. Hauser, *Muhammad Ali: His Life and Times*, p.406.
3. Pacheco, p. 19.
4. Michael Katz, "Holmes Stops Ali and Keeps Heavyweight Title," *The New York Times*, October 3, 1980, p. A28.
5. Hauser, *Muhammad Ali: His Life and Times*, p. 397.
6. Dave Anderson, "Ali's Decision: This is the End," *The New York Times*, December 13, 1981, Section 5, p. 4.
7. Hauser, *Muhammad Ali: His Life and Times*, p. 430.
8. Ali and Hauser, p. 6.
9. Miller, p.132.
10. Ibid., p. 84.
11. Phil Marder, "The Hall of Fame Opens Its Doors to Ali," *Ring*, October 1987, pp. 12-13.
12. "Forty For the Ages," *Sports Illustrated*, September 19, 1994, pp. 49.
13. William Plummer, "The World's Champion," *People*, January 13, 1997, p. 43.
14. Miller, p. 75.

For further information

Books

Ali, Muhammad, and Thomas Hauser. *Healing: A Journal of Tolerance and Understanding.* San Francisco: Collins, 1996.

Anderson, Dave. "Ali's Decision: This is the End," *The New York Times*, December 13, 1981, Section 5, p. 4.

Bonventre, Peter. "Fool's Gold," *Newsweek*, April 7, 1975, p. 59.

Bottjer, Eric. "The 10 Greatest Controversies in Boxing History," *Ring*, March 1997, pp. 27–47.

Brady, Dave. "Ali Remains Evasive on Retirement," *The Washington Post*, September 17, 1978, p. F1.

Denlinger, Kenneth. "Project-Raised Spinks Can't Wait to Travel," *The Washington Post*, February 17, 1978, p. C3.

"Forty for the Ages," *Sports Illustrated*, September 19, 1994, pp. 46–147.

Gates, Henry Louis, Jr. "The Charmer," *The New Yorker*, April 29/May 6, 1996, pp. 116–131.

Gorn, Elliot J., editor. *Muhammad Ali: The People's Champ*. Chicago: University of Illinois Press, 1995.

Gutteridge, Reg. *Boxing: The Great Ones*. London: Pelham Books, 1975.

Haley, Alex, and Malcolm X. *The Autobiography of Malcolm X*. New York: Ballantine, 1965.

Hall, Kermit L. *The Oxford Companion to the Supreme Court of the United States*. New York: Oxford University Press, 1992.

Haneef, Suzanne. *What Everyone Should Know About Islam and Muslims*. Des Plains, IL: Library of Islam, 1993.

Haskins, James, and Kathleen Benson. *The 60s Reader*. New York: Viking Kestrel, 1988.

Hauser, Thomas. *Muhammad Ali: In Perspective*. San Francisco: Collins, 1996.

_____. *Muhammad Ali: His Life and Times*. New York: Simon & Schuster, 1991.

Katz, Michael. "Holmes Stops Ali and Keeps Heavyweight Title," *The New York Times*, October 3, 1980, p. A28.

133

Kindred, Dave. "Atlanta Games," *The Atlanta Journal*, July 21, 1996, p. 34S.

_____. "He'll Always Be the Greatest," *The Sporting News*, July 29, 1996, p.6.

Klose, Kevin. "Ali in Moscow," *The Washington Post*, June 20, 1978, p. A1.

MacHt, Norman. *Muhammad Ali*. New York: Chelsea House, 1994.

Marder, Phil. "The Hall of Fame Opens Its Doors to Ali," *Ring*, October 1987, pp. 12–13.

Mathews, Jack. "Ali's the Greatest, and So Is the Movie," *Newsday*, October 25, 1996, p. B17.

Miller, Davis. *The Tao of Muhammad Ali*. New York: Warner, 1996.

Nack, William, "The Fight's Over, Joe," *Sports Illustrated*, September 30, 1986, pp. 52–67.

Pacheco, Ferdie, *Muhammad Ali*. New York: Birch Lane, 1992.

Plummer, William. "The World's Champion," *People*, January 13, 1997, pp. 40–47.

Polenberg, Richard. *One Nation Divisible: Class, Race, and Ethnicity in the United States Since 1938*. New York: Penguin, 1980.

Riley, Rochelle. "Muhammad Ali: Coming Home," *Louisville Courier-Journal*, December 3, 1996, p. 1A

Sammons, Jeffrey T. *Beyond the Ring: The Role of Boxing in American Society*. Chicago: University of Illinois Press, 1988.

Schudel, Matt. "Past With a Punch," *Fort Lauderdale Sun-Sentinel*, October 15, 1995, p.12.

Schulman, Arlene. *Muhammad Ali: Champion*. Minneapolis: Lerner, 1996.

Shenon, Philip. "At Baghdad's Bazaar, Everyone Wants Hostages," *The New York Times*, November 27, 1990, p. A17.

_____. "Defiant Iraq President Declares He Is Ready to Fight the U.S.-Led Forces," *The New York Times*, November 20, 1990, p. A11.

Smith, Gary. "Ali and His Entourage," *Sports Illustrated*, April 25, 1988.

Stravinsky, John. *Muhammad Ali: Biography*. New York: Random House, 1997.

Suster, Gerald. *Champions of the Ring: The Lives and Times of Boxing's Heavyweight Heroes*. London: Robson, 1992.

Videotapes

The Thrilla in Manila from NBC Sports Greatest Fights Ever series.

When We Were Kings, directed by Leon Gast, 1996. This Academy Award–winning documentary on the Rumble in the Jungle is the best video account of Ali's career.

Internet Sites

Muhammad Ali: The Making of a Champ
http://www.courier-journal.com/ali/
Provides a listing of Ali-Cup events as well as biographical information of Ali and a photo gallery.

Muhammad Ali: The Greatest Web Site
http://www.theslot.com/ali/index.html
Gives details on Ali's record and provides a photo gallery. Also offers an assessment of heavyweight champions.

Yahoo! Recreation: Boxing
http://gnn.yahoo.com/Recreation/Sports/Boxing/
Lists fight schedules, reviews, and results. Provides promoter and manager directories, fighter profiles, and links to other boxing sites.

Index

About the Author

John Tessitore is an assistant editor at *Maxim* magazine and a regular contributor to the *Christian Science Monitor*. He is the author of *The Hunt and the Feast: A Life of Ernest Hemingway*, also with Franklin Watts.